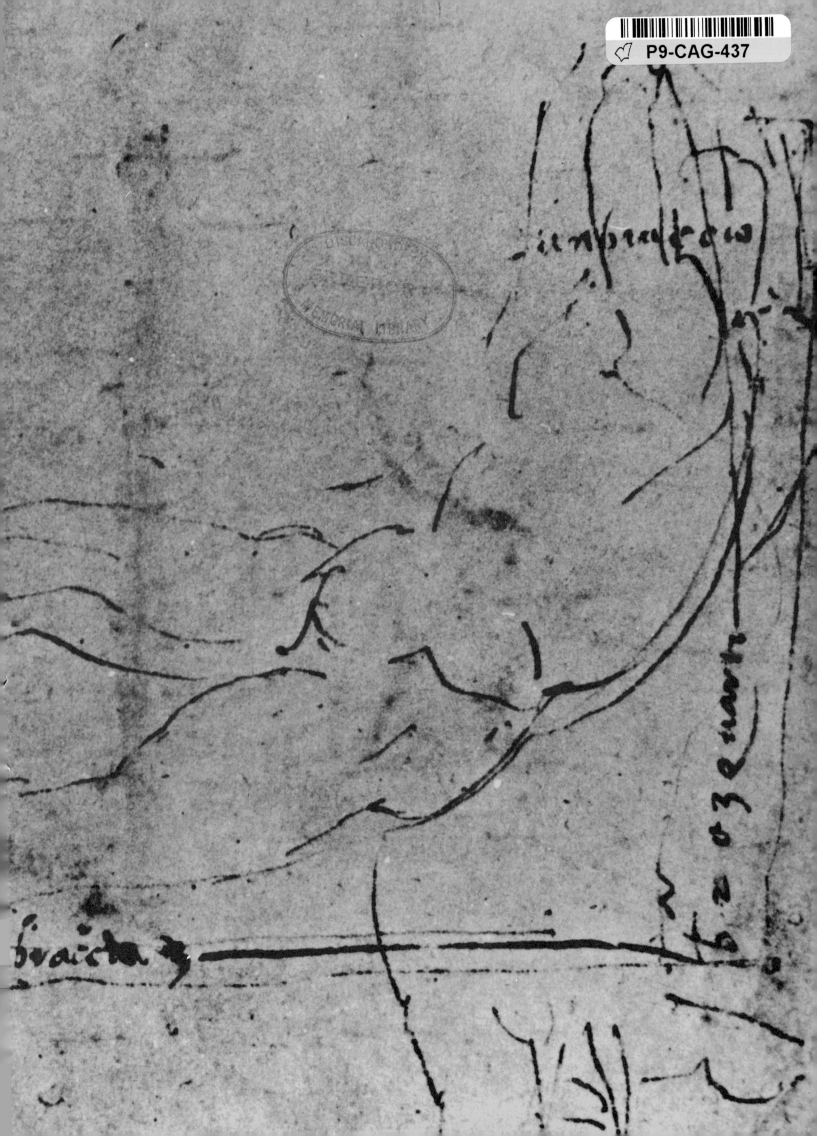

Michelangelo Models
formerly in the
Paul von Praun Collection.
Dedicated with many thanks to
the author's wife, Phyllis, and
to his twin brother, Peter.

Michelangelo

Models *formerly in the*

Paul von Praun Collection

by Paul James LeBrooy

Creelman & Drummond Publishers Ltd., Vancouver, Canada

A Torso of a Youth—terracotta model, in the Vancouver Collection, about 1489. (*Opposite*)

Contents

Introduction

With the exception of Ludwig Goldscheider's *A Survey of Michelangelo's Models in Wax and Clay,* the present volume (published approximately 60 years after Henry Thode's Catalogue of Michelangelo's models) is the only modern work on extant models by the Great Master. Many of the one hundred and eighty-three reproductions in the book show remarkable details and illustrate exciting aspects of the terracotta models which were formerly in the famous von Praun Collection in Nuremberg, Germany. The relationship of these clay models to drawings and to many of the marble statues by Michelangelo, in particular to those in the Medici Chapel, is shown with unmistakable clarity.

The volume is unique in that it is constructed somewhat along the lines of a lecture. It is not analytical but rather synthetical. Those who prefer to read a page here and there will not derive full benefit, as the reader should proceed right through the book in order to better appreciate the very remarkable historical references and to understand the ideas incorporated in it. Then only will the author's schematic approach become apparent. The reader will be taken back to an early period of modelling in clay, then into the Renaissance, and on into Michelangelo's workshop where he will be informed as to how models were made and employed by Michelangelo.

One section of the book makes it clear that wax and clay studies were also used by Michelangelo for his paintings — the same models which at other times were employed for sculpture. There are also important sections which explain how Michelangelo was influenced by the *Antique*, especially in his early years.

A most interesting chapter in the volume covers a number of points which the author is confident will rectify numerous and long established misconceptions about Michelangelo, and which will bring the reader up to date regarding past research on models by him. Although complete clay statuettes such as the *Phases of the Day* for the Medici Tombs are of great importance, the author points out that models of torsos and of single limbs, such as legs and arms and hands, are also mentioned in the old sources and shown in drawings by Michelangelo, in opposition to the view of some scholars who are inclined to place value only on complete statuettes by Michelangelo, as they consider limbs and torsos to be copies.

The many illustrations of the models which were formerly in the von Praun Collection, in particular those now in the Canadian Collection, show how these small pieces of clay sculpture were employed again and again by Michelangelo in a number of different positions and for various purposes through a period of years. Thus the reader will visualize the actual use of models and realize their importance in understanding the works and the genius of Michelangelo.

Chapter I

The historical use of clay models
for artistic purposes

1 Side view of two Cypriotic terracotta figurines, 7½ inches high, in the Vancouver Collection, *Cypro-Archaic* period, 7th century, B.C.

2 Frontal view of the two clay figurines (offerings found in a shrine of ancient Cyprus), in the Vancouver Collection.

Because clay is the simplest and most easily worked medium for sculpture, it has been used by man from the beginning of his history as a means of expressing his artistic ability through the making of models (Figs. 1 & 2).

It was not until the discovery of the art of drying and of firing malleable clay that it became possible to preserve almost indefinitely, in the form of terracotta, what the fingers and modelling stick had previously shaped. The sculpturing of small terracotta figures, the most spontaneous of technical methods, has contributed to most civilizations a popular way in which human and animal forms, and inanimate objects can be represented in miniature and in full scale. Wet clays useful for modelling are abundant throughout the world and they differ in colour and fineness of texture from region to region. Before the figures are moulded by hand they are prepared and freed from impurities and are often retouched by an assortment of blunt, sharp-pointed, or rounded instruments. When the early sculptors finished the modelling of the figures, often household gods, they then allowed them to dry for a period.

Clay which is unbaked and air-dried or sun-dried, is called "terrasecca", but clay which has been fired and baked in a kiln is known as "terracotta". Terracotta models are often judged the most beautiful and fascinating works of art on a small scale. These sculptures, by virtue of the flexibility of the material used, escape from the limitations which bind statuary in stone and which prevent them from attaining a similar suppleness and familiarity of life. The clay used in figures, which have been formed with the object of firing them, has unusual and special attributes which provide the finished products with a great variety of colours and textures, especially when handled by artists who are sensitive to the charms of the clay matière. Colour can range from a soft grey to that of an earthy red, and the texture can be as smooth and brittle as a china dish or as coarse and unbreakable as a building brick.

Greek terracotta models are considered by many as the most charming of all small sculpture made prior to the Renaissance period, in that the figurines achieve the most unaffected naturalism and the most refined beauty. The most celebrated group of terracotta figurines which antiquity has left to us are those discovered in the tombs of Tanagra in Boeotia, Greece. These small statuettes, designed to accompany the dead in their tombs, most often represent gracious maidens and were produced in moulds. It is of interest to note, that the Greek sculptors of the early and finest periods, worked directly in the marble only with the aid and guidance of a small sketch or study in clay. It was not until the latest Greek period, about the first century B.C., that there is evidence of the practice of previously modelling the figure or group in full size in clay.

The use of terracotta during the Renaissance

Terracotta as an artistic medium appears to have been used very rarely after the fall of the Roman Empire and was not again extensively employed until the later period of the Middle Ages, when it was used primarily for architectural decoration rather than for individual pieces of sculpture. With the coming of the Renaissance, the use of terracotta by artists took on an increasing importance and thereafter it was constantly employed. Free sculpture in terracotta found its revival in fifteenth century Italy, and undoubtedly the finest expressions in this field of creative art were produced in Florence. During the course of the fifteenth and sixteenth centuries almost every sculptor of note in Italy (Fig. 3) worked in terracotta in some form or other.

Terracotta sculptures by Jacopo della Quercia, Donatello, Verrocchio, Antonio Pollaiuolo and Giovanni da Bologna, that have survived to this day, show the liveliness, realism and artistry which can be achieved in this medium. Many terracottas of the

3 Sculptors and Pupils of the *Academy of Baccio Bandinelli in Rome,* studying small male and female models. Engraving by Agostino Veneziano, 1531, London, British Museum.

11

period were intended to be fully realized works of art and they are striking in their faithfulness to the rendering of personal characteristics less frequently found in other sculpturable media such as marble. They exhibit a quality which is impossible to transfer to the sterner material, as so many of the clay compositions were intended to be studies, created by the sculptor in the heat of artistic inspiration. On the other hand, many were highly finished terracotta models on a small scale which were used to assist the artists in creating works directly in stone or bronze, in the hope of rivalling the sculptors of antiquity.

Michelangelo Buonarroti (1475-1564), in particular, made use of terrasecca and terracotta, in addition to such other media as wax, as an intermediary stage in the creation of his monumental sculptures in marble. Examples of his small models are found today in the Casa Buonarroti in Florence, Italy, where terrasecca is to be found in the main, and in the Vancouver Collection in Canada, where all the models are of terracotta. He also made large scale clay models for many of his intended works in marble. The only extant model of this type, however, is the seventy-inch model for a River God (Fig. 134), presently in the Casa Buonarroti. Michelangelo appears to have made many, many drawings as well as models. Vasari (1511-1574), the noted painter and biographer of Michelangelo, attributed Michelangelo's superior grasp of foreshortening, and of light and shade, to his use of models. He further added that being immobile, the wax and clay models had the advantage over living models. Undoubtedly he used many small models while in the process of painting the "Last Judgment", for there are many postures in it which no living model could maintain for more than a few

seconds. A study of Michelangelo's models and of many of his drawings, along with those by artists of the sixteenth and seventeenth centuries which have reproduced Michelangelo models, is most instructive.

Giovanni da Bologna (1524-1608) at a comparatively young age brought to Michelangelo, then in his eightieth year, a model which he had finished with infinite care, but the Master, passing his fingers over it, altered every part, saying, "Learn to sketch before you attempt to finish".

When wax models are dipped into warm water, they become pliable, therefore Michelangelo made use of their pliability to twist and alter the positions of the models for use in various poses in his paintings and sculptures.

Vasari, in his 1568 biography of Michelangelo, outlined a sculpturing technique used by the Great Master when he carved the four rough hewn "Captives", formerly in the Boboli Gardens and now in the Accademia in Florence. His method was to take a figure of wax, or other firm material, and immerse it in a vessel of water. As the carving of the marble proceeded, normally from the front, the model was gradually raised, first exposing the uppermost parts, the rest being still hidden beneath the level of the water. As each part of the stone statue was carved, the model was again raised, until finally the model was wholly exposed, coincident with the intended total or part completion of the marble sculpture.

Benvenuto Cellini (1500-1571) in his graphic memoirs stated that Michelangelo generally worked with a small model, as in the case of a wax model in the Casa Buonarroti, Florence (Fig. 4). This model was used by Michelangelo for one of the figures in the "Last Judgment", according to Ludwig Goldscheider (*A Survey of*

4 A Wax Model for a *Slave* or a *River God*, in the Casa Buonarroti, Florence, about 1540.

Michelangelo's Models in Wax and Clay, figs. 3 and 5). Umberto Baldini states (*The Complete Work of Michelangelo*, p. 122) that it is a model of a "River God"—agreeing with Goldscheider's alternative. Other uses to which he put models, as well as drawings, were in submitting sculptural concepts to a patron, or in assisting the buyer of marble in his dealings with the stonecutters. The use of models also enabled him to turn over parts of the final sculpture or painting to his assistants.

A number of the all too few models by Michelangelo in existence show in a clear manner the perfect harmony existing between Michelangelo's brain and hand. This relationship is more apparent in clay than in many of his marbles, which in some part were carved or polished by assistants working under his direction. In the opinion of the art historian, Ludwig Goldscheider, models by Michelangelo are easier to understand and more exciting than most of his drawings. Michelangelo was foremost a sculptor, not a draftsman, and his models show us his first ideas for his statues, sometimes more inspired than many of his sculptures on which he laboured for so many years.

When a comparison is made with the finished marble sculpture, a number of the small models demonstrate the importance and the manner in which these preparatory works were used by the Master. The com-parisons are most remarkable with respect to models in terracotta of parts of the human anatomy because they show the way in which parts of the body were conceived and how they were used by Michelangelo to express his ideas in the small format. Models of single limbs, such as legs, hands and arms, are in accordance with his and other workshops of the period. Drawings executed by Michelangelo also show that a study of the parts of the human body was a specialty of his work method. Plastic models were made by him for various purposes and he used them more than once. For the frescoes on the Sistine Chapel altar wall and on the ceiling, Michelangelo made not only drawings and cartoons but also models in wax and clay, and therefore it is often difficult to ascertain whether a certain model (Fig. 4) was originally made for a piece of sculpture or for a mural painting. Charles de Tolnay, an eminent authority on Michelangelo, notes on p. 26 of *The Complete Work of Michelangelo* that: "It also happens sometimes that a figure he had conceived in his youth reappears reversed in a later work, but always in a more developed form. For instance, the 'Hercules' of his youth (which we know from the model in the Casa Buonarroti and an ink drawing by Rubens) was developed in reverse nine years later in the marble 'David'." Figures 159 and 157 in Chapter V of this present volume show the model and drawing referred to by de Tolnay. Giovan Battista Armenini in 1587 gave a description of Michelangelo's method of painting when models in wax and clay were used, and stated: "As we all know, one or two figures in full relief contain an endless number of views and we have just to turn those models round and round in order to find those views and use them in our painting." Small round holes for suspension purposes were often made in the models by sculptors in order to obtain the variety of views required. Giovan Armenini quotes Michelangelo as saying that he often made models for his works and checked them against the subject when they were completed. With reference to his sculpture, Michelangelo believed that the models themselves must have a perfection of their own, as they are the pledge of the beautiful form to emerge from the stone, as promised by the hammer.

For each large or full-scale model which Michelangelo made there were at least two small models. The first being simply a slight sketch, which when combined with a drawing (Fig. 5) showed the dimensions of the marble form to be sculptured, and served as a guide whereby the stonecutter was able to cut out the marble block required. The only extant small model in this rough style is the one in wax for a reclining male figure which is now in the British Museum (Fig. 135). As already mentioned, the second type of small model was specifically fashioned by Michelangelo in wax or clay as an intermediary stage in the creation of many of his monumental works in painting and in marble.

Michelangelo's models on a small scale, especially the highly finished terracotta models, appear to have been greatly in demand by collectors during the creator's lifetime, and although he personally destroyed many of them while he was alive a number have survived. In his day, the esteem in which Michelangelo was held by his countrymen can be ascertained from the following passage of a letter dated January 20, 1538, to Michelangelo from Pietro Aretino, a prominent and powerful writer and journalist of his time who later turned against Michelangelo. Aretino wrote as follows:

"Does not my devotion deserve that I should receive from you, the prince of sculpture and painting, one of those cartoons which you fling into the fire, to the end that during life I may enjoy it, and in death carry it with me to the tomb?"

Aretino, six years after the date of the above letter, wrote again to Michelangelo in April, 1544:

"Why will you not repay my devotion to your divine qualities by the gift of some scrap of drawing, the least valuable in your eyes? I should certainly esteem two strokes of the chalk upon a piece of paper more than all the cups and chains which all the kings and princes gave me."

It is reported that Pietro Aretino was beside himself with joy over a small wax model that Michelangelo had made for the head of Saint Cosmas in the Medici Chapel and which had come into his possession. Vasari proudly related that he had numerous models made by the Master himself in his house in Arezzo. There is no artist of the Italian Renaissance of whom we possess as much evidence of continuous modelling in wax and clay, as we do of Michelangelo. Vasari, discussing this point in detail, wrote a special chapter on the manner in which models for sculptors were to be produced in wax and clay. He expressly stated that nobody knew better than did Michelangelo how to use models in wax and clay for his works. In his *Veri Precetti*, Armenini puts

5   Working Drawing for a Figure, by Michelangelo, with indications in his handwriting of measurements for a marble block, in the British Museum, London, 1525.

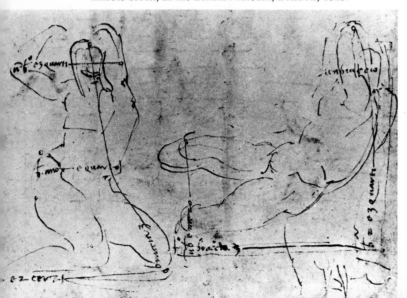

these words into Michelangelo's mouth: "I have always made models for all my works".

According to the earliest biographers, Michelangelo, while still in his teens, worked in the garden of San Marco, where he made small terracotta figures under the direction of his teacher, the celebrated sculptor Bertoldo di Giovanni (1420-1491), and a marble head of a faun (now lost) after an antique model which Lorenzo de'Medici, the "Magnificent", had admired. Vasari, in his *Life of Michelangelo*, 1568, reports that when Michelangelo arrived in the garden of San Marco he found his fellow student Pietro Torrigiano (1470-1528) modelling clay figures, as his teacher Bertoldo had ordered him to do. Michelangelo watched him for a little while, and then immediately made some of his own in competition.

The Venetian architect and sculptor Allessandro Vittorio (1525-1608) was pleased to acquire, in 1563, directly from a Bologna art dealer named Nicolo Zolfino for three Venetian skudi, a single clay model by Michelangelo. The model acquired was a small sketch for the left foot of the "Day". In a letter of 1517 (Carl Frey, *Michelangelo Briefe,* 1907, p. 85) Michelangelo speaks of a small model in terracotta for the facade of San Lorenzo which he had made for his own use and which had lost its shape "like a butter cake."

The great Venetian painter Tintoretto (1518-1594) possessed a number of small Michelangelo models, of which one was a model for Giuliano de'Medici in the Medici Chapel, Florence, as is known from numerous drawings. There is a drawing by El Greco (1541-1614) which is now located in the Munich Print Room and which is after a lost Michelangelo model.

According to Cellini, it was the practice of Donatello (1386-1466) to work from the small study, and that Michelangelo started his career as a sculptor on the same system. His colossal statue of "David" was carved, according to Vasari, with the sole aid of a small model.

In 1531 Antonio Mini, a favourite pupil of Michelangelo, went to France, and in order to pave his future welfare there, Michelangelo gave him a large number of drawings, the tempera painting of "Leda and the Swan" which has since been lost, and two large boxes full of models—see de Tolnay *The Medici Chapel*, Vol. III, p. 190, where he mentions the gift of "terracotta" models. Mini died in France and all his treasures must have been scattered. The Florentine sculptor Giovanni Rustici (1474-1554), however, returning from a trip to Paris, brought back a few of these models to Florence. As the clay models which Michelangelo gave to Mini were meant to be transported over a considerable distance, they could not have been slight and friable terrasecca sketches, but rather detailed productions with the artistic value of terracotta models.

It is also of interest to note that since wax models are unsuitable for transportation, and that small models and drawings were required in order to arrive at the outline of a figure which was eventually to be carved in stone, Michelangelo must have travelled with clay models so that he could obtain the correct size and shape of the marble block required from the quarries of Carrara.

In 1533 Michelangelo summoned the sculptor Tribolo (1485-1550) to Florence from Loreto and gave him the allegorical figure of "Earth" and "Heaven" to work on for the Medici Chapel. In October of that year he made two small models for Tribolo and they were probably for these two allegorical figures (*Milanesi*, p. 470).

The importance to Michelangelo of the small model in its relationship to sculpture and painting was demonstrated by Battista Cavalieri in 1574 when he carved the marble statue, "The Allegory of Painting". This statue (Fig. 6) is a part of the Tomb of Michelangelo in the Church of Santa Croce, Florence, and it shows a model of a nude male held by the female figure, thus emphasizing Michelangelo's use of models during his lifetime.

6
The Allegory of Painting holding a model by Michelangelo. Marble by Battista Lorenzi del Cavalieri, 1574. A detail from the tomb of Michelangelo in the Church of Santa Croce, Florence.

16

Chapter II

The difference between wax, terrasecca and terracotta models

Material for sculpture is only suitable if it can withstand the test of time and of the elements. For this reason the materials suitable to sculpture are limited to stone, non-ferrous metal, fired clay, and to wood—the least durable. Historically, the weaker materials, such as wax and unfired clay, have been used as a means of making forms which were later to be reproduced in a more durable substance or else were made into figures with an intentionally short life.

WAX

Wax has frequently been used as a final medium, for the making of models (Figs. 4, 159 and 169). In such cases, however, the complete sculpture should be put under glass or some similar protection should be given in order to preserve it from changes in temperature and from damage. Wax, as a positive form, is also often used as a vehicle to make the negative form (clay or plaster cast) of a piece of sculpture. As a moulding material, wax is very useful for casting delicate shapes which otherwise might be harmed through the chipping action of a hammer or chisel.

Michelangelo is known to have made plaster and clay casts of very finely executed wax models. There is a stucco cast, "Descent from the Cross", in the Casa Buonarroti, which was made from a lost wax relief by Michelangelo; his student Leone Leoni (1509-1590) also made casts from a number of Michelangelo's sketches in wax. A wax relief by Michelangelo was the basis of Leoni's "Michelangelo Medal" in bronze. The principle of moulding is similar in all kinds of casts, and involves the making of a negative (female) mould of plaster or clay from which the positive original (wax or clay) can be removed, and into which the casting medium (wax, clay or bronze) is introduced in order to make the final positive form desired. Figures 4, 159 and 169 show wax models by Michelangelo in the Casa Buonarroti, with their altered surfaces now showing little of the original fine workmanship of their creator. It would appear, with due consideration given to the iron spike protruding from the head of one of the models (Fig. 159) and the faint seams appearing along its length, that this particular model was cast in a mould with the hot wax having been poured through an opening into the cast. Generally speaking, a figure which is to be made in a mould must be rather simple in its overall shape.

Plaster or clay casts of very finely executed wax models were undoubtedly also used by Michelangelo to make some of his models in terracotta. On the wax model was brushed a thinly diluted wash of clay which was then allowed to dry. Successive coats of clay were then applied until the wax model was completely surrounded by a firm covering of clay. The new model in clay which was then formed in the clay cast, or sections of the cast, was less vulnerable to breakage than the original wax model and on its surface it showed the same perfection of form as the wax model which had previously been melted away in an oven during the process of hardening the clay mould. The final result was a clay model in one or more sections showing all the initial detailed artistry, patience, care and skill lavished by Michelangelo on the original wax model. Where there was more than one section of the cast, prior to firing the complete clay model in a kiln and during the hardening stage of its clay, the separate parts were joined with the seams having been moistened and the joints sealed by the use of a wooden modelling tool in order to smooth and weld the edges firmly together. It is known that Michelangelo made a number of large and small bronze figures and therefore he must have been quite familiar with the art of casting, and he must also have been quite familiar with the technique of firing a kiln. E. Müntz in his lengthy article of 1895 titled *Les Collections d'Antiques Formées par les Mèdicis au XVI^eSiècle*, catalogues under the year 1553 the following art object: "Un torso di bronzo ritratto da un 'Fiume' di mano di Michelangelo."

CLAY

Undoubtedly the most easily available material for sculpture that can be found is clay. It is of the same origin as the igneous stone which a sculptor carves, in that it is the end product of stone, decomposed due to weathering. The decomposed particles, having been washed away by the rains, are subsequently laid down where streams and rivers assume a slower course. In some places these deposits of moist and cohesive earth are particularly fine and it is from these deposits that clay is dug and used for making pottery and terracotta sculpture.

Clay used for sculpture does not have to be as fine and pure as that used for pottery, unless it is intended that the clay be ultimately fired. Any type of clay can be used to make a cast. Clay used for casting which is to be fired in a kiln, however, should be as fine as possible and free from sand and any hard particles that might harm the cast.

As the clay model starts to dry it goes through a leather-hard stage, in which the clay is still damp but no longer plastic, and if the sculptor should try to squeeze the model into a different shape he will succeed only in breaking it. As the drying process continues, all the water plasticity will leave the model and the clay will become bone-dry.

A considerable amount of shrinking takes place while the clay dries. If the drying is so uneven that one part of the model shrinks faster than another, then the model will warp and crack. If one part of the model is thin and another thick, the thinner part may become bone-dry while the rest of the piece is still damp and as a result it will break off. To avoid cracking or breaking, the clay model should be allowed to dry as slowly and as evenly as possible. As clay dries out at the top, a moistened cloth should be placed over the top of the model while the lower portion must be left uncovered.

Two or more clay pieces may be joined together if they have the same moisture content. If, however, one of the pieces is drier than another there will be unequal shrinkage and the joint will not hold. When two pieces are to be joined, the areas that fit together should be roughened and then moistened with water or slip before being pressed firmly together with the joint welded with a wooden modelling tool. Although it is not a difficult matter to join two pieces of clay when they are plastic or even when they are in the leather-hard state, the joining of bone-dry pieces is indeed very difficult.

Of the twenty to thirty extant models which have been generally accepted by most authorities as being by the hand of Michelangelo, a few are in wax and the rest are in clay of either terrasecca or terracotta. In the course of the four hundred years since

7 A Terrasecca Figure, a model for an allegorical female figure, in the Casa Buonarroti, Florence, about 1525-1530.

the time of Michelangelo, the surviving wax models have lost, in part, their original form and shape and portions of them have since been reshaped by a hand other than that of Michelangelo. The frail terrasecca clay models (Figs. 7 and 10) have also deteriorated over the years and have been broken, chipped and cracked in many places, due in large part to hot or damp atmospheric conditions affecting their rather porous structures. Many extant wax and terrasecca models ascribed to Michelangelo by a number of art historians are in fact too sketch-like and so damaged that positive attributions are unwarranted. For example, the wax sketch (Fig. 169) without arms in the Casa Buonarroti that de Tolnay now states, on p. 65 of *The Complete Work of Michelangelo,*

was made by Michelangelo for the "David", and the wax model of "The Young Boboli Giant" in the Victoria and Albert Museum in London which Sir John Pope-Hennessy says, on p. 422 of Vol. 2 of his *Catalogue of Italian Sculpture in the Victoria and Albert Museum,* that the balance of probability is in favour of it being by the hand of Michelangelo, whereas most of the other living art historians now consider it to be a copy of the marble statue.

There is a great difference between terracotta and terrasecca. Even at the early stages of choosing and preparing the clay, Michelangelo would have had to decide which of his models were to be fired (terracotta) and which were not to be fired (terrasecca). One of the problems of a terracotta sculpture is in allowing the chemically combined water to escape from the clay during the process of firing. If a model is heavy and the clay dense, the water will not escape quickly enough and will be turned into steam which will explode the model. In small models this can be prevented by adding "grog" to make the clay porous. Grog is previously-fired clay which has been ground up and screened to workable size. When the ground-up clay is mixed with the pliable clay, porosity is provided, enabling the chemically combined water to escape. Figures to be modelled in clay must be bone-dry before being subjected to the intense heat of the kiln. As in drying, the clay will shrink during the firing process, and if one part dries more rapidly than the rest it will crack and break away. It is therefore necessary to maintain a nearly equal thickness and avoid solid masses of clay of which the outer layers, drying more quickly, will shrink and crack. The sculptor is forced to adopt somewhat complex methods when he wants to do work in the round. Very small figures can be fired successfully when solid, but larger works have to be hollowed out before firing. To be safe, any clay model more than a few inches tall, especially those to be fired in a kiln, should be hollow. If a mould is not to be employed, a piece of ceramic sculpture can be hollowed out by allowing the clay to become leather-hard and then slicing it in two and scooping out each half. A shell of even thickness should be left all around. For larger pieces the shell can be up to three-quarters of an inch; however, for small models the shell should be considerably thinner. As already stated, when the halves have been hollowed out, the cut edges should be moistened with water or clay slip, and the two parts pressed firmly together. The joint should be sealed by using a wooden modelling tool, so that wherever possible no sign of a crack remains and the edges are tightly welded. If necessary, some of the clay scooped out of the centre can be used to wedge into the joint. It should also be noted that a piece of clay sculpture need not be cut into two in order to hollow it out, as this can often be done by scooping out its interior from the bottom or back of the sculpture. A wire loop tool or knife with a curved blade is the proper type of instrument for this purpose. Michelangelo was undoubtedly able to make many of his smaller pieces of clay sculpture without cutting them in two, simply by scooping out the clay material from the bottom or back of the model.

It is possible to fire small solid clay models, if it is done slowly enough, if the clay body is strong enough, and if the clay has been compacted sufficiently so as to be free from air pockets and impurities. For best results, however, the clay model to be fired should be made hollow with a hole or holes to release expanding air during the firing. As ceramic sculpture is hardened by fire, the sculptor must understand the effects of heat upon his clay material, know how to operate a kiln and how to measure its temperatures. Remarkable changes take place in clay when it is subjected to heat. When clay is fired in a kiln the weathering process which created the substance is reversed and in a few hours the clay is changed back into a material very similar to the original rock from which it was formed.

All clay can be fired provided it is clean and free from all foreign bodies which might react unfavourably to the clay and its natural components during the firing process. Foreign bodies, such as plaster of paris or iron particles, will cause the fired clay to crack, and small holes will also appear on the surface during and after the firing. The kinds of clay most suitable for making sculpture to be fired are those used by potters, and the colour of the clay most readily available is normally red or white.

A kiln is an oven made in such a way that when heated very slowly, the heat will circulate evenly around every clay object placed inside it, until the desired maturing temperature of the clay is reached. The maturing temperature varies with the type of clay to be fired. An earthenware firing may mature at any temperature between 1000°C to 1100°C, and stoneware firing may mature between 1250°C to 1350°C. The temperature is maintained at the maturing rate for a short time and then cooled down as slowly as it was previously heated. Sudden heating or cooling will cause cracking. The construction and the operation of a kiln is quite complicated, as are the procedures to be followed in the preparation of the ceramic pieces of sculpture to be fired.

Terracotta will withstand almost all of the ravages of time and weather. It will not rust as iron does, nor will it disintegrate as

8   The Back Side and Left Thigh of a Reclining Figure, terracotta model, in the Vancouver Collection, about 1524.

does cement or plaster. It will even outlast many kinds of stone or marble. Unglazed terracotta sculpture weathers beautifully, like brick, and it will not lose its original colour through the years but acquires a patina with the passing of time. Terracotta models (Fig. 8) by Michelangelo are as good and in as fine a condition as they were when they were made by him over four hundred years ago, in that unlike his porous, soft, and sun-dried terrasecca models (Figs. 7 & 10), they are extremely hard and impervious to weather or extremes of temperature.

The difference is apparent in the terracotta model (Fig. 9) and the terrasecca model (Fig. 10) by Michelangelo. Any comparison between them is as invalid as that between a marble sculpture of the 16th century and a wood sculpture of the same period. The

techniques used and the results differ far too radically for comparative purposes.

During the period of the Renaissance, majolica (tin-glazed ware) potters were spread all over Italy. In the orbit of the Medici there was located a majolica pottery in Caffagiolo, near Florence. Donatello, Verrocchio, Jacopo della Quercia, the della Robbia brothers and nephews, Tintoretto, Tribolo, and of course Michelangelo, are just a few of the prominent Renaissance sculptors who have left their work in terracotta. It would therefore appear that it was not very difficult for Michelangelo to obtain the appropriate type of majolica clay and to have his models fired.

The majolica potters used several different clays which they carefully mixed to obtain the consistency most suitable for

21

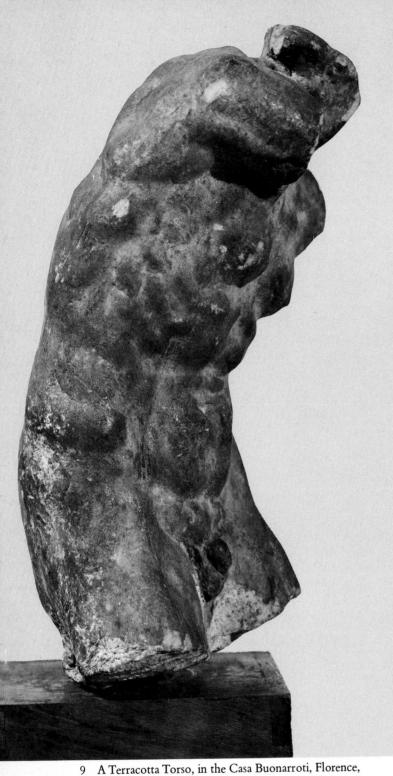

9   A Terracotta Torso, in the Casa Buonarroti, Florence, about 1534-1536.

10   A Terrasecca Group, model for a Victory Group, (*Hercules and Cacus*) in the Casa Buonarroti, Florence, about 1528.

modelling and firing. It is evident, that to create his models, Michelangelo used the same clay as did the majolica potters of Italy and indeed if he did not personally do, or at least supervise, the firing of his own models, it could not have been difficult for him to have others do the firing for him.

In summary, it would appear that Michelangelo made most of his models directly in clay, with the thicker models being cut with a curved knife for hollowing-out purposes. The interior carving was especially necessary where the models were later to be fired in a kiln. A number of small models were originally made in wax, and from these plaster or clay casts were made to obtain the final clay models, which were then fired.

Chapter III

The Paul von Praun Collection

Art throughout the ages has been the means of raising the status of its owners and adding lustre to their name. This custom began on a fairly large scale with the Ptolemies in Egypt. It continued in Greece and in the palaces of Imperial Rome, and was re-awakened in the courts and great homes of the nobility in the period of the Renaissance and its aftermath. In the same manner that Alexander summoned the great painter Apelles, so also did the Medici in Florence, the Popes of Rome and the Holy Roman Emperors summon the leading artists of their time to their courts. The nobility, the Church and the emerging middle class were all eager to possess the creations of these artists.

Mankind owes private collectors an incalculable debt, as without them many of the world's greatest works of art would never have been created nor have been preserved to this day. Public art collections are to a very great degree simply private collections which have been accumulated and combined. It is a well-known fact that the more a national or municipal art gallery rests on the acquisition of one or more private collections (i.e. the Hermitage and the Prado), the greater is the resultant quality, and the more it is the creation of a museum official the more arid it is. It is not trade unions nor municipal councils, nor other emanations of the popular will, which have encouraged talented artists or have saved great works of art for the people, but rather a number of extraordinary individual collectors of the past. These collectors and preservers of the cultural heritage of man have in most cases been ruthless, greedy, tyrannical and disreputable in many ways. They have all had one common quality, however: the principle of delight in collecting, wherein each purchase was a vivid experience, very often culminated only after a long pursuit or a struggle in which economy and prudence were superceded by an unquenchable desire to possess a particular piece of art.

The alliance of business and the arts goes back to early civilizations. In the past many wealthy merchants have succumbed to the seduction of beauty and art in their private lives, and have experienced the refinements of culture, which except through the acquisitions of war can be obtained only through commerce and trade. Many of them, such as the Medici of Florence who were the patrons of Michelangelo, commissioned poets, sculptors and painters in order to add lustre to their reputations and beauty to their homes. During the Renaissance, in Florence and in a number of the commercial cities of Northern Italy such as Bologna, the financial and merchant princes were invariably aggressive in their pursuit of wealth, and yet they were almost always appreciative of beauty in all its forms and sensitive to the arts and culture of their own environment as well as those of other countries. The majority of these businessmen were very literate and highly cultivated—characteristics developed by the need to successfully run large silk and wool plants in Italy and abroad, to finance domestic and foreign business and banking enterprises, and to deal with the nobility and merchants throughout the then-known world. Not only was the culture and the art of Italy introduced into the trading spheres of these businessmen, but they brought back with them the art productions of many of the renowned Flemish and German painters and engravers. Their activities in the field of cultural resources were not unlike those of the late nineteenth and early twentieth century U.S. financial magnates such as Hearst, Frick, Mellon, Morgan, Rockefeller and Guggenheim.

Nuremberg, Germany, during the Renaissance was also a centre of all forms of artistic activity, and for a considerable part of that time her influence in art and industry alike was a preponderant one. Some of the very best of the private collections in Germany were those owned by a number of wealthy merchants and industrialists in Nuremberg. These collections, particularly that of Sebald Schreyer (1466-1520) and those of Paul von Praun (1548-1616) and Wilibald Imhof (ca. 1550) were typical in character and content with the other great private collections in Europe, but because of Nuremberg's position as the centre of the munitions industry of Europe and one of its great commercial centres, they were probably, except for some notable exceptions, more costly and of finer quality than others in Europe at that time. The von Praun Collection was very rich in bronzes and it contained an extraordinary collection of gems and precious and semi-precious stones, and a very large selection of coins and medals. Paul von Praun, besides being an ardent collector of paintings and sculpture, also acquired during his journeys in Europe, particularly in Italy, a very large number of drawings, engravings and small terracotta models.

Adolph Donath (ca. 1920) on p. 58 of his "Psychologie des Kunstsammelns" stated:

"One of the most magnificent private collections of Nuremberg which reached back into the 16th century, was the Praun Family Collection. It included, along with the Italian and German Masters of the 16th century, a rich collection of bronzes—reputedly 81—over 2,000 gems and a large range of coins. Paulus Praun (1548-1616) was moreover a passionate collector of drawings. He had a complete collection of Dürers and acquired during his journeys to Italy very rare cartoons by Raphael, Michelangelo and Correggio."

Paul von Praun was born in Nuremberg on October 23, 1548, and died in Bologna on July 8, 1616. His father was Stephen von Praun, and his mother's maiden name was Ursula Ayer. He was descended from a branch of the Bruns or the Brunis, from Zurich, who, dating back to 1187, were important members of the Town Council. The father (Stephen II von Praun) gave his younger son Paul, as well as his elder son Stephen III (1544-1591), very thorough educations and both were encouraged to travel extensively. Stephen III travelled in 1569 with Count von Minkwitz, an important member of Maximilian II's court and his ambassador at Constantinople, and journeyed extensively in Spain, Portugal, France, England and the Low Countries. On April 29, 1591, Stephen III died in Rome. His brother Paul lived the life of a philosopher and remained a bachelor and he was at all times interested in classical books and studies. These human qualities found their outward expression in his enthusiastic pursuit of collecting many forms of art. During Paul von Praun's frequent associations with the finest artists of the day he received a great deal of advice, acquired an extensive knowledge of art, and applied it during the acquisition of his collection in Nuremberg as well as in Bologna, Italy, a town where he lived for much of his lifetime, and which was a centre of major art-dealing during the sixteenth and seventeenth centuries. Paul von

Praun's collection of drawings by Dürer was considered the best of its day, and it is of interest to note that he managed to acquire a number of the famous drawings which Vasari had collected. The following is an extract from p. VII of Christophe Theophile Murr's 1797 catalogue of the von Praun Collection:

"Il divisoit les soins pour ses collections entre Nuremberg et Bologne. C'est en ce dernier lieu qu'il faisoit acquision d'une grande partie des débris du fameux recueil de dessins du 'Vasari' qui son héritier avoit apporté de Rome; et c'est de cette collection que sont entrés dans le Cabinet de Monsieur Paul de Praun plusieurs dessins de Raphael, de Michel-Ange et d'autres grands maîtres."

Vasari, living at the time of von Praun, is known to have owned small Michelangelo models and, indeed, clay sketches by Michelangelo for the head and the arms of "Cosmas" in the Medici Chapel were regarded by Vasari as invaluable gifts. The art historian Christophe Theophile Murr (1733-1811), the author of *Bibliothèque de Peinture, de Sculpture et de Gravure* in 1770, and also of *Leben des M.A. Buonarroti,* stated in his 511 page catalogue of the von Praun Collection *Description du Cabinet de Monsieur Paul de Praun à Nuremberg,* 1797, that von Praun acquired in Bologna at the end of the sixteenth century, the remainder of the famous Vasari Collection of drawings which Vasari's nephew and heir, Chevalier George Vasari, had brought from Rome. Murr was of the opinion that from the Vasari Collection many drawings by Michelangelo and Raphael and by other great masters found their way into the collection of Paul von Praun.

A small forty-two page volume titled "Michelangelos Tonmodelle aus der Haehnel'schen Sammlung", published privately after Henry Thode's and Professor Lehnert's writings on the Haehnel Collection in 1913, makes an interesting but very possibly unverifiable statement:

"Most important, Vasari, the author, painter and architect, kept a catalogue which was published after his death, in which there is a notation saying that the models which Vasari had left behind were bought from his heir by Paul de Praun in Bologna in 1598."

It should be noted that the above extract does not state that those models purchased by von Praun from Vasari's heir were necessarily by Michelangelo. The von Praun Collection contained models by many sculptors besides Michelangelo.

Von Praun was throughout most of his lifetime surrounded by a close circle of acclaimed art connoisseurs and famous artists of the day, especially during the periods of his life that were spent in Bologna and in Nuremberg. In his youth he was the close friend of Springli of Zurich and of the engraver and woodcarver Jodocus Amman, as well as of the goldsmiths Albert and Christoph Jamnitzer. During his lifetime he was an intimate friend of Lucas van Valkenborch, Peter Schaubruck, Giovanni da Bologna, Denis Calvaert, Annibale Carracci, and many other artists. The advice of Praun's artist friends and their associates was at all times available to him in order that he might increase his collection of outstanding art, obtained for the most part in Italy and in Germany.

By the year 1589, von Praun had in Nuremberg a very fine collection of paintings, drawings, busts, terracottas, bronzes, medals and medallions, engraved precious and semiprecious stones, gems, ivories, copper engravings, woodcuts, and many rare books and manuscripts. Amongst the nobility, his associates included Johann Friedrich the Elector of Brandenburg-Onaldbach, Count

Jerome de Scotti, the Duke von Holstein, Count von Oettingen, and many other personages of high rank.

In 1597, as recorded in the Murr Catalogue, he received the following letter written at the dictate of the Hapsburg Emperor Rudolph II (1552-1612), with respect to his desire to obtain several paintings from von Praun for his own collection. Rudolph was the greatest collector of his age, his agents ransacking Europe to fill his museums with rare works of art. His desires in this case, however, were unfulfilled as von Praun did not wish to part with the requested art treasures.

Sir,

It is by the order of his Imperial Majesty, our very gracious sovereign, that I ask you that his worthy Majesty having a desire to make a collection of beautiful, rare and first rate paintings, and knowing that you are a great connoisseur of these unparalleled masterpieces of the Italian and Flemish masters and others which you have set about to collect, in which manner you have had perfectly good success. He has charged me, Sir, that I pray you that I bring to him that which you have of excellence of Michelangelo, of Raphael, of Parmigianino or of Correggio, of which masters His Majesty has not as yet acquired very much. He has the intention of giving you in place of these some rare and precious stones, for example jasper and others or some rare diamonds of which you could not be otherwise than very satisfied, as Herr Nitgel, instructed by His Majesty, will tell you this. You will do, Sir, that which you will find appropriate. Written in Prague, May 1st, 1597.

Yours
very affectionately, your servant,
Jean P. Heydon

Von Praun's collection of 250 paintings was of such quality, that it included two paintings by Michelangelo, two by Raphael, one by Leonardo da Vinci, two by Andrea del Sarto, one by Guido Reni, two by Tintoretto, ten by Albrecht Dürer, one by Peter ("the Droll") Brueghel and one by his son Peter ("Hell-fire") Brueghel, two by Titian, seventeen by Denis Calvaert, and many, many others including paintings by Dosso Dossi, Vasari, Caravaggio, Parmigianino, Mantegna, Lucas Cranach, and Jacob Jordaens.

Two paintings by Dürer ("John the Baptist" and "St. Onuphrius") from the von Praun Collection are presently located in the Bremen Kunsthalle, and two other Dürer paintings from this collection are to be found in the Munich Alte Pinakothek ("A Portrait of a Young Man"—probably Dürer's brother Hans) and in the Germanisches Museum in Nuremberg ("Portrait of Michael Wolgemut" —Dürer's teacher). In the National Gallery, Washington, D.C. there is a very fine portrait in oil of the clergyman Johannes Dorsch which was painted in 1516 by Dürer on vellum mounted on wood. This signed painting, which has lasted without a blemish, was formerly in the Paul von Praun Collection; the Count Johann Rudolf Czernin von Chudenitz Collection, Vienna; the Czernin Gallery, Vienna, and in the Samuel H. Kress Collection, 1952. This portrait was possibly among the works by Dürer which von Praun bought from the heirs of Wenceslas Jamnitzer, who had in turn acquired them from Andre Dürer, the younger brother and heir of the famous artist.

Donath, in his "Psychologie des Kunstsammelns" writes:
"Included among the von Praun pictures were, as C.F. Neickel (ca. 1727) mentions, two by Amberger, which represent the Portraits of "Emperor Charles V" and of "Sebastian Munster" the well known cosmographer." Both portraits are the most important works of Amberger and are presently located in the former State Museums in Berlin. Christoph Amberger (1500-1561) was a student of Hans Holbein, and

26

Charles V was of the opinion that his paintings were comparable to those of Titian.

Joachim von Sandrart in his *Akademie* (P.II; Vol. 3, p. 235) states that the Emperor paid triple the price that Amberger had previously asked to paint his portrait, the price being a chain of gold with a portrait locket of the same metal. This portrait of the Holy Roman Emperor Charles V was painted in 1532 when Charles was age 32, and was purchased by Praun in Bologna in 1585 from a German named Jean Kinig, who was also a friend of Giovanni da Bologna.

In the Schlossmuseum at Gothe, Germany, there is a portrait, "Hieronymus Holzschuher" painted in 1578 by Hans Hofmann, the renowned Dürer copyist and court painter to Rudolph II. This portrait and thirty-four other paintings by the same artist were formerly in the Praunsche Kabinett (The von Praun Collection in Nuremberg).

The very large collection of drawings formed by Paul von Praun was undoubtedly one of the finest to be found in Europe in its time. It contained eighteen drawings by Michelangelo, three by Denis Calvaert, five by Annibale Carracci, four by Domenichino, eight by Dosso Dossi, thirty by Guilio Romano, four by Andrea Mantegna, twenty-nine by Raphael, fifteen by Albrecht Dürer, four by Andrea del Sarto, four by Albrecht Altdorfer, twelve by Parmigianino, four by Lucas Cranach, fifteen by Martin Schongauer, five by Tintoretto, and many, many others, including drawings by Vasari, Lucas van Leyden, Guercino, Primaticcio, Correggio, Titian and Veronese. There are presently in the Budapest Museum of Fine Arts many fine drawings from the von Praun Collection, and foremost among them are some drawings from Schongauer's workshop, including "Annunciation", which is characteristic of that artist's power of com-

position. Important drawings in the Budapest Museum from the von Praun Collection are two sketches by Dürer. One of them, titled "Various Sounds" appears to be inspired by Erasmus's satire. The other, "Sallies", of an angel making music, is a work by Dürer which is imbued with his Italian memories. Also to be found in this museum are drawings by Baldung Grien and Altdorfer which were formerly in the von Praun Collection.

The Praunsche Kabinett contained in excess of four thousand seven hundred copper and wood engravings amongst which were two hundred and ninety-one (and four engraved copper plates) by Hans Sebald Beham; two hundred and forty-nine by Heinrich Aldegrever; one hundred and five by Lucas van Leyden; forty-seven by Lucas Cranach; one hundred and eighty-six by Albrecht Altdorfer; one hundred and sixty-two (plus one engraved copper plate) by George Pencz; forty by Augustin Hirschvogel; thirty-four by Marcantonio Raimondi and thirteen by Martin Schongauer. The Murr Catalogue under Portfolio "B" of the engravings contains a listing of four hundred and sixty-two prints which are the individual works of Hendrik Goltzius and Jacob Matham. The Catalogue gives a description of a large percentage of the engravings listed and among the artists mentioned appear such names as Agostino Veneziano, Marco da Ravenna, Cornelius Matsys, Michel Wolgemut, Hans Baldung Grien, Hans Schaufelein, Virgil Solis, Jacques Androuet du Cerceau, Hans Bol, Marten de Vos, Hans Lautensack, the brothers Jerome and Lambert Hopfer, Giulio Bonasone, Andrea Mantegna, Agostino Carracci, and Parmigianino. The Kabinett held perhaps one of the finest collections ever acquired of Albrecht Dürer's engravings (104 from copper plates and 350 from woodcuts) all of the "first state", and these were bought by von Praun from the heirs of Wenceslas Jamnitzer who had obtained them directly from Albrecht Dürer and from his younger brother Andre, from which source two Dürer wood blocks and an engraved copper plate by Martin Schongauer also came into the von Praun Collection. Schongauer, who executed approximately one hundred and fifteen prints during his lifetime, was one of the truly great German artists. One of his masterpieces is the "Temptation of St. Anthony", and an impression of this plate was much prized and copied by Michelangelo. The Murr Catalogue contains a detailed description of this famous engraving by Martin Schongauer and also lists the same subject among the drawings by him in the von Praun Collection. Today's value of von Praun's collection of engravings is indicated to some degree by the fact that in 1965 a very fine Dürer engraving "The Knight, Death, and the Devil" was purchased for over seven thousand dollars, and in 1968 his "Melancholia" was sold at Sotheby's for almost five thousand pounds. Both of these impressions from copper plates, as well as the world-renowned third master-engraving "St. Jerome in His Study", were in the von Praun Collection. The fifteen woodcuts of "The Apocalypse" were only a part of the many famous woodcuts by Dürer among the 350 listed in the Murr Catalogue.

Today, if a museum were to own eight bronzes by Giovanni da Bologna they would be considered to be rare and prized possessions. Among the 122 bronzes listed in the Murr Catalogue of the von Praun Collection there are eight by Giovanni da Bologna and four by Johann G. van der Schardt.

Some idea as to the value of the drawings in the von Praun Collection can be gained from the fact that it contained one drawing by Leonardo da Vinci, eighteen by Michelangelo and twenty-nine by Raphael. A Raphael drawing ("Madonna and Child with the Infant St. John") was purchased in 1964 by the Metropolitan Museum in New York for a little over eighty-nine thousand dollars.

Among the 250 paintings in the Praunsche Kabinett there were two by Michelangelo, two by Raphael and one by Leonardo da Vinci. The "Portrait of Ginevra die Benci", a panel painted by Leonardo da Vinci about the year 1483, was purchased in 1967 by the National Gallery in Washington for a price which is said to be in excess of fourteen million dollars. A painting by Michelangelo, if it were available for sale today, would bring an almost unbelievable price at auction. In view of the fact, however, that there now exists only one easel painting by Michelangelo ("The Madonna Doni" in the Uffizi Gallery in Florence) a monetary evaluation can never be put to the test.

Paul von Praun lived much of his lifetime in Bologna where he owned a silk factory. As early as the late 1580's distinguished visitors to Nuremberg insisted upon viewing the portion of the von Praun Collection located in that city and collected by von Praun for the most part in Italy. In the year 1616 at the age of sixty-eight, having decided to prepare for his retirement in his homeland, he sent that part of his priceless collection which still remained in Bologna to Nuremberg, having founded there a perpetual "Family Trust" for its preservation. Unfortunately, before he could move to his fatherland, death overtook him and he died on July 8, 1616, in Bologna and was buried at the Monastery Church of the Holy Sisters Katharina de Strada Maggiore. Two days before his death he had allotted a sum of money for the erection of a chapel over his grave and to commemorate his birth date. The chapel is situated on the left hand side of the church on proceeding through the main portal. On the left hand side of the altar is to be found the marble bust of Paul von Praun, as well as that of his nephew, Heinrich von Praun, who died in 1626, according to the Latin inscription.

Engraving of Paul von Praun by Jean Nussbiegel in 1795, after a painting of Paul von Praun by Lorenz Strauch in 1598.

Chapter IV

The history of the Michelangelo Models in the von Praun Collection to the present day

During the 17th and 18th centuries the von Praun Collection, known as the Praunsche Kabinett of Nuremberg, was the most valuable of all the art collections in southern Germany. The Collection was famous throughout Europe, and until 1797 it was visited by persons of outstanding rank. Cabinets similar to, but perhaps of lesser fame than, the von Praun and the Imhof Collections in Nuremberg were by no means uncommon during the 17th century, as they were a reflection of man's sudden awakening to art, science, and nature in the late Renaissance. Both the von Praun and the Imhof Collections have long since been dispersed, but the Amerbach Kabinett in Switzerland was spared such a fate. When an Amsterdam art dealer wished to buy the collection from the Amerbach family, the Senate of Basle intervened and in 1662 bought it for a considerable sum, jointly with the University in whose care it was left. As a result, the city of Basle came to possess a veritable treasure of the works of Holbein and the first public art collection as distinguished from one owned by a ruling royal house. The continuous wars of the 17th century resulted in additional costs to the governments involved, and even Emperor Rudolph II had to sell many of the art treasures he had accumulated at the Hradschin Palace in Prague. Nevertheless, the love for art was kept alive in Nuremberg and during the 17th and 18th centuries the von Praun Collection continued to withstand the disturbances of the times until the 19th century, because of the restrictions regarding its sale laid down under the terms of the perpetual "Trust".

Owing to the Thirty Years War (1616-1648) there is no record of the Collection during that period. There are a number of references to the von Praun Collection made by Johann Keyssler (1693-1743) during the course of his *Voyages* (Vol. 2 of the 1751 edition). Keyssler was of the opinion that, because Rome was plundered in 1527 during Emperor Charles V's reign (1500-1558), Praun was subsequently, over the years, able to salvage many pieces of art which had been scattered over Europe. In 1766, von Will, professor of philosophy at Atldorf University, Germany, mentions the Collection during his discourses in his "Nuremberg Munzbelustigungen". From the list of drawings in the Murr Catalogue it is possible to estimate that there were around 1,000 drawings in the von Praun Collection, of which approximately one-half (many with appropriate descriptions) are ascribed to specific artists, with the balance simply listed in unspecified multiple amounts under a number of general catagories. The Catalogue gives a detailed list of 59 of the drawings which were engraved by Johann Gottlieb Prestel (1739-1808) in the years 1780 and 1782. The "Freymuthiger Catalogue" with its 36 engravings by J. G. Prestel contains reproductions and descriptions of eleven which he made of drawings in the Praunsche Kabinett. The 1802 "Frauenholz Catalogue" of drawings from the von Praun Collection details under nos. 1551-1561 those that were formerly engraved by Prestel.

From the time that Paul von Praun declared, just before his death in 1616, that his art collection as well as his house on the Weinmarkt in Nuremberg, should be in a perpetual "Trust" and until the Collection was broken up in 1801, nothing was added to it. At the beginning of the 19th century Lieutenant-Colonel Friedrich von Praun, the then eldest member of this famous Nuremberg family, wrote the following in the 3rd volume of his family's chronicle in the Munich Archives, relative to the issue in 1797 of a catalogue of the Collection by Christophe Theophile Murr:

"The creation of a catalogue was done mainly to have a record for an eventual sale of the Collection. Murr delivered on the 22nd of June, 1796, the manuscript of the catalogue of the Collection after he had worked on it for 20 years, and he did not receive the 10% of the eventual purchase price, as he had arranged with the previous owners. Instead he received only a lump sum payment of 1,200 Florins and 1,000 copies of the catalogue were printed. The French invasion of Germany followed and times were very critical for the Collection. The French Inspector General Dumouriez viewed the Collection without any results. However in April, 1797, the French having withdrawn from Nuremberg, merchant Buttner and the art dealer Jean Frederick Frauenholz from Nuremberg opened negotiations with regards to the purchase of the Collection. These negotiations were only completed after four years, namely on the 20th of April, 1801. The total inventory of the Praun art collection was then sold to the two above mentioned gentlemen, Buttner and Frauenholz. An art collector, von Derschau, was also involved."

Christophe Theophile Murr's Catalogue in 1797 (*Description du Cabinet de Monsieur Paul de Praun à Nuremberg*) of the von Praun Collection contains over 500 pages, of which 270 pages relate to the description of marbles, terracottas, ivories, bronzes, engraved stones (precious and semi-precious), coins and medals (in gold, silver, bronze and lead) and precious and semi-precious uncut gems. Two hundred and thirty pages deal with paint-

ings, drawings, copper engravings and woodcuts. The first 35 pages of the catalogue are concerned with paintings, and these are listed with their height and width detailed in most cases in feet and inches. Under no. 98 of the Index for pictures, there is a description of a painting on canvas by Michelangelo, 1ft 9in. high, by 10in. wide, being a study of "Haman" for the ceiling of the Sistine Chapel in Rome. The Catalogue also contains the same subject in a terracotta bas-relief, 10in. high, by 5in. wide, by Michelangelo—Model no. 76, as well as in no. 233 in the copper engraving Portfolio C inspired by the same artist. In no. 225 of the Index for pictures, there is a description of a painting of a "nude youth" on canvas by Michelangelo, 2ft 1in. high, by 1ft 8in. wide.

Among the drawings listed in 30 pages of the Murr Catalogue, there are many by the old masters, of which eighteen are ascribed to Michelangelo. A listing of the copper engravings and woodcuts follows that of the drawings and there are 163 pages of these classified, many of which are by or after the famous Italian, Dutch and German masters. This very extensive listing includes 34 by Marcantonio Raimondi, 47 by Lucas Cranach, and 105 by Lucas van Leyden. It is in turn followed by an enumeration of the bronze and marble busts, as well as reliefs— many of which were in alabaster. A description of some, but not of all the terracotta models, as well as that of many ancient Greek and Roman medals, is to be found in Murr's Catalogue, and finally the last 22 pages are devoted to a listing of the old books and manuscripts forming part of the Collection.

The terracottas listed are of special interest in that nos. 29, 30, 31 and 32 are the four terracottas by Michelangelo which are stated on p. 241 to be the models for the

"Day", the "Night", the "Evening" and the "Dawn" in the Medici Chapel. With reference to these four models, the Catalogue mentions that the clay model for the "Night" was damaged. Murr also mentions on p. 241, under nos. 41 and 42, two terracotta models of prisoners (slaves) by Michelangelo, and these, it can be assumed, are for the two "Slaves" of the Julius Monument (now in the Louvre, Paris). On p. 243 under nos. 100 and 149 are various terracotta models of torsos and parts of the human body. Some of these sketches are, as in the case of the already referred to nos. 29-32, models for the statues in the Medici Chapel; some are models for other well-known statues by Michelangelo; some are sketches by the Great Master which are not particularly defined, and some are studies after the "Antique" or of a character according to the "Antique".

According to the Murr Catalogue, as listed in 140 pages, the von Praun Collection contained a remarkable collection of gems, cameos, and engraved precious and semi-precious stones of which 1,169 are detailed and all of which are from old Roman, Etruscan, Greek, Egyptian and Arabic sources. Medallions and coins in sundry metals from various ancient Roman and Greek regions and cities (and bearing likenesses of famous personalities of their times), as well as a precious library of rare books and manuscripts, were also substantial parts of the Collection.

It is apparent from the von Praun family chronicles that the contemplated sale of the Collection was primarily motivated by the Napoleonic Wars and by the political situation in Nuremberg at the close of the 18th century. The complete collapse of the Austrian state finances at the end of the century was the final factor in the decision of the descendants of Paul von Praun to disregard the wishes of the founder of the Art Collection and to thwart his original intent that the Collection should never be sold and that it should belong inalienably to his descendants. The art collector von Derschau had some of the art in the Collection set aside for his own personal enjoyment, whereas merchant Buttner and art dealer J.F. Frauenholz (1758-1822) were primarily interested in the Collection from the point of view of a resale and the resultant profit.

The collection of drawings, prints and books which Frauenholz bought from the von Praun family was listed in a catalogue issued by his firm in the year 1802, and by 1803, to the immeasurable loss of the city of Nuremberg, almost the entire Collection, with the exception of some drawings and the terracotta models by Michelangelo and one terracotta plaquette which were kept by Frauenholz, was sold to Prince Nikolaus Esterházy (1765-1833). Of interest is the fact that there is a drawing by Albrecht Dürer in Munich (Graphische Sammlungen, Inv. no. 13) which is recorded as having been acquired in 1810 by Crown Prince Ludwig von Bayern from the Praunsche Kabinett. When the von Praun art acquisition by Esterházy (consisting of 647 pieces) was brought from Vienna, it filled 14 rooms— there were 194 works of art from the Italian School; 33 from the Spanish School; 82 from the German School; 279 from the Dutch School and 59 from the French School. In 1855, the painter Joseph Altenkopf was found guilty of theft and sale of much of the Esterházy Collection with a large part of the remainder being heavily damaged. In 1821 it had been known as one of the greatest collections in Vienna (F. H. Bockh, *Wiene Lebende Schriftsteller, Kuenstlet, etc.*, Vienna, 1821, p. 298 ff). In *Peintre Graveur*

Wien, 1808, Vol. VI, p. 17, Adam von Bartsche stated that the Collection of Prince Esterházy was one of the most significant in the city. In 1870 the remnants of the Esterházy Collection, having been acquired by the State of Hungary, were moved to Budapest where they are now displayed in the Museum of Fine Arts. Of great current pride to the city of Budapest is the beautiful series of drawings by the greatest German painters and their followers, which was formerly in the von Praun Collection and which is now in its Museum of Fine Arts. A detailed history of the Esterházy Collection can be found in Dr. Simon Meller's *Az Esterházy Keptar Tortenete,* Budapest, 1915.

In or about the year 1803 the Michelangelo terracotta models, the terracotta bas-relief and the terracotta plaquette in the von Praun Collection passed from Frauenholz into the possession of the well-known dealer in art, Lieutenant-Colonel von Gemmingen of Nuremberg, and in the year 1842, all or most of the models and the plaquette were sold by von Gemmingen (or by his estate) to the famous sculptor and architect Ernst Julius Haehnel (1811-1891) of Dresden. Julius Grosse in his publication of 1893, *Ernst Julius Haehnel's literarische Reliquien* wrote:

"There were to be found in Haehnel's estate various objects of art which are noteworthy—foremost of which were the famous terracottas by Michelangelo that Haehnel had discovered one day in an art collection in Nuremberg. It was a transaction concerning a Madonna that had brought him to see von Gemmingen's possessions. The Madonna had been sold the day before. Then Haehnel discovered terracottas covered with dust, the style of which caught his attention. Another look, and he at once recognized his favourites from San Lorenzo in Florence. How was that possible? Authentic Michelangelos in the middle of Germany! Upon further research he found, according to the catalogue, that they came from a Bolognese

Collection which had been brought to Nuremberg. They were indeed the original models for the famous 'Phases of the Day' which Michelangelo later completed for the monuments in San Lorenzo. To be sure, only three figures: 'Day', 'Night', and 'Dawn', whereas 'Evening' was missing. As complementary pieces to the aforesaid there were torsos, little feet and hands and other portions of the human body. These valuable relics have still not been sold. A considerable sum of money is said to have been offered for them in England."

The renowned art historian Henry Thode (1857-1920) stated in an article written in 1913 ("Michelangelos Tonmodelle aus der Haehnelschen Sammlung", in *Monatshefte für Kunstwissenschaft,* VI) that if Professor Haehnel did not buy from von Gemmingen all the terracotta models in the von Praun Collection, which is very likely, then he must have bought most of them. It should be noted however, that a beautiful small terracotta model for the "Medici Madonna" was originally in the von Praun Collection and until 1869 also in the Haehnel Collection which year Haehnel sold it to the Kaiser Friedrich Museum in Berlin where it remained until towards the end of World War II when it was smashed into splinters. Unfortunately, only the very small unbroken head remains. Haehnel in 1875 exhibited his complete collection of Michelangelo models at the Fine Arts Building of the Bruehlsche Terrasse in Dresden (A. Gutbier, *Katalog der Michelangelo-Ausstellung . . .,* Dresden, 1875). In the same year, at the large exhibition in Florence commemorating the fourth centenary of Michelangelo's birth, a substantial number of the models were exhibited by Haehnel (Carl von Lützow, "Die Michelangelo-Ausstellung in Florenz", 1876). These included the models for the "Day", the "Night" and the "Dawn" in the Medici Chapel—the model for the "Evening" which was formerly in the von Praun Collection, as detailed in the Murr Catalogue, had long since been lost and it was never in the Haehnel Collection. Besides the three models for the "Phases Of The Day" (Figs. 11, 38 and 59) for the Medici Monuments, there were exhibited from the Haehnel Collection of models by Michelangelo, one sketch of the lower body of "Christ" (Fig. 110) and eight others, including a torso sketch for the "David" (Fig. 120) and parts of the human body. Figure 31 was also illustrated by Lützow. Carl von Lützow states in his *Zeitschrift für Bildende Kunst*, 1876, that the models from the Haehnel Collection were the best pieces at the exhibition because they are the only ones in the world. It is reported that the Collection was one of the "hits" of the exhibition and that Haehnel was escorted in triumph to his train in an open carriage bedecked with flowers. There are many interesting references in the well-documented history of the Haehnel Collection. For instance, Professor Haehnel received numerous offers from interested collectors and even Queen Victoria tried without success to acquire his collection of terracotta models by Michelangelo. Henry Thode and Meier-Graefe reported that Haehnel took great delight in showing the models to all interested German artists and scholars, Peter von Cornelius (1783-1867) being one of them, and they, with the same passionate admiration as his own, shared his opinion that they were an extremely valuable treasure. Cornelius was a well-known German artist who studied in particular the school of Raphael, Michelangelo and the "Antique".

At the death of Professor Haehnel in 1891, the Collection of models by Michelangelo, originally from the von Praun Collection, was inherited by his wife, Frau Elise Walter Haehnel and then by his daughters Anna and Elisabeth Haehnel in Dresden. It appears that in 1913 there was a legal dispute regarding their ownership or perhaps their inheritance. The litigation definitely involved value, as on April 3 of that year, a seventeen-page opinion titled "Expert Opinion on Models by Michelangelo" was submitted by Professor Dr. George Lehnert at the request of the Royal Courts of Berlin. In his opinion, Professor Lehnert pointed out that he was not asked to give his opinion as to the authenticity of the models but only as to their value. Even without going directly into the genuineness of the Collection as coming from the hand of Michelangelo, he placed its value at 1,472,680 Marks. It is of interest to note that the German Mark was worth 23 cents in 1913, and therefore the Collection was valued at that time by Dr. Lehnert in the amount of $338,716.

In or about the year 1922 the Collection of terracotta models by Michelangelo passed from the estate of Ernst Haehnel into the hands of the South West African Trust Company Limited.

Sometime after 1924, in which year the art critic Julius Meier-Graefe published in Berlin his monumental and now very rare work, *Michelangelo, Die Terrakotten Aus Der Sammlung Haehnel* and which included a very large portfolio of 40 excellent photoengravings (a number from different angles) of the individual models by Michelangelo in the Haehnel Collection, the Collection passed into the ownership of Dr. A. B. Heyer, who then sold it at public auction at Christie's of London. This sale took place in 1938 shortly before World War II, at a time when there was a tremendous slump in the art market owing to the impending Continental war.

From the time that Paul von Praun

formed the Collection of models, not so many years after the death of Michelangelo (von Praun was age 16 at the time), and during a period when he was in an excellent position to ascertain their origin and genuineness, until 1938 when the Collection was sold as individual pieces at Christie's, the Collection remained intact for the most part, and in the hands of private owners. At the Christie's sale, of the thirty-three terracotta models which were sold to seven different buyers, over one half (17 models) are now in the Vancouver Collection in British Columbia, Canada. The Vancouver Collection is also referred to as the "Canadian Collection" in the text of this volume. It is known that four models (the "Night", the "Dawn", "The Right Arm of Christ" in the Pietà in St. Peter's and "The Right Hand of Moses") are presently in the Victoria and Albert Museum in London, and one model (the "Day") is in the Museum of Fine Arts in Houston, Texas. There is also a terracotta plaque from the von Praun Collection (sold at Christie's at the same time as the models) in the Morgenroth Collection at the Museum attached to the University of California. This plaquette was attributed by Ulrich Middledorf on a questionable basis to Prospero Sogari, but according to the noted art historian, Ludwig Goldscheider, it is actually by Leone Leoni after a wax design by Michelangelo (*A Survey of Michelangelo's Models in Wax and Clay,* fig. 61). It was illustrated as the frontispiece of the excellent catalogue of the "Sigmund Morgenroth Collection of Medals and Plaquettes" during the course of the exhibition at The Art In-Institute of Chicago, in 1944.

There are therefore eleven models from the Haehnel-von Praun Collection which were sold in London in 1938, of which the whereabouts are unknown at present date. These missing models went to various buyers at the Christie's sale and it is possible that they have been destroyed or lost during the course of the bombing and ravages of the war which commenced shortly afterwards. Interest in the von Praun Collection is therefor enhanced by the thought that one or more of these missing models may yet come to light at some time in the future.

In correspondence between the author of this volume and Sigmund Morgenroth prior to his death in 1963, Mr. Morgenroth made the following, as yet unchecked, statement:

"You may be interested to know that at the Christie auction in 1938 a Paris art dealer, Dr. von Frey, acquired one of the larger of the small models and resold this model for a very high price to an Australian museum."

Chapter V

Models by Michelangelo in the Haehnel-von Praun Collection

Group I

Models for the statues in the Medici Chapel

Group II

Models for other well-known statues by the Master

Group III

Studies by Michelangelo after the "Antique" or of a character according to the "Antique"

A bas-relief by Michelangelo

A plaquette after a design in wax by Michelangelo

Group I

Models for the statues in the Medici Chapel

The *Dawn*

Height 7in. 178mm.
Length 8½ in. 218mm.

The model of the "Dawn" (Fig. 11) which is now in the Victoria and Albert Museum in London, is slightly different from the finished marble (Fig. 12) in the Medici Chapel in Florence. It is, however, a perfect masterpiece on a smaller scale, and an excellent illustration of Michelangelo's initial inspirational ability, as he progressed from the model to the final marble statue. The head, the left arm and the lower right leg of the model (Fig. 13) are missing,

11 The *Dawn*—terracotta model, in the Victoria and Albert Museum, London, about 1524.

38

12
The *Dawn*, marble statue in the Medici Chapel, Florence, about 1524-1531.

13
The *Dawn*—terracotta model, in the Victoria and Albert Museum, London.

and there is considerable damage on its back. There are firing cracks through the right thigh and elsewhere in the model. The drapery under the upper right thigh is built in a more bulky manner in the model than in stone, and the bearing of both figures differs somewhat. In the marble statue the abdomen is raised a little higher and directed a little more towards the spectator, whereas the model shows the abdomen to be in a more recumbent position

14
The *Dawn*—terracotta model,
in the Victoria and Albert
Museum, London.

(Fig. 14). This indicates that Michelangelo made an important change after completing the model as in the finished statue he intensified the impression of the figure by enhancing the movement.

The small rectangular base of the model must have been added between 1913, a year when it and the model for the "Day" and the "Night" are not shown with bases in Henry Thode's illustrations of the models, and the year 1924 when Meier-Graefe published his photo-engravings of the three "Phases of the Day" in the Haehnel Collection ("Evening" had long since been lost—it was never in the Haehnel Collection), all of which showed the addition of a base to each of the three models. Since the acquisition of the models for the "Dawn" and the "Night" by the Victoria and Albert Museum, the bases have been removed. The interior clay of the model was probably scooped out by Michelangelo through a hole in the base of the model, or it is quite possible that this model, and those for the other "Phases of the Day", may have been sliced into two or more parts for hollowing-out purposes with the separate parts being rejoined, prior to the complete drying and firing processes.

Although damaged as a result of the firing, there exists a very close relationship between the back view of the terracotta model of the "Dawn" (Fig. 15), and that of the marble sculpture of the "Dawn" in the Medici Chapel (Fig. 16). The comparisons are not exact, however, because the model has been sculptured by Michelangelo on a more complete and slightly altered basis than that employed by him when he carved the statue in stone. The back of the marble is rough-hewn in parts and less sculptured than the one in clay, especially beneath the stone figure, and at the rear of its left foot where its view is concealed by a raised portion of the stone base. It should also be noted that the downward continuation of the figure's head-dress is considerably more defined at its back in clay than it is in marble, as is the modelling beneath it.

For the many reasons stated, it is obvious that the terracotta figure of the "Dawn" in the Victoria and Albert Museum must be an earlier creation of Michelangelo's original sculptural conception than his marble statue in the Medici Chapel.

15
The *Dawn*, the back of the terracotta model in the Victoria and Albert Museum, London.

16
The *Dawn*, the back of the marble statue in the Medici Chapel, Florence.

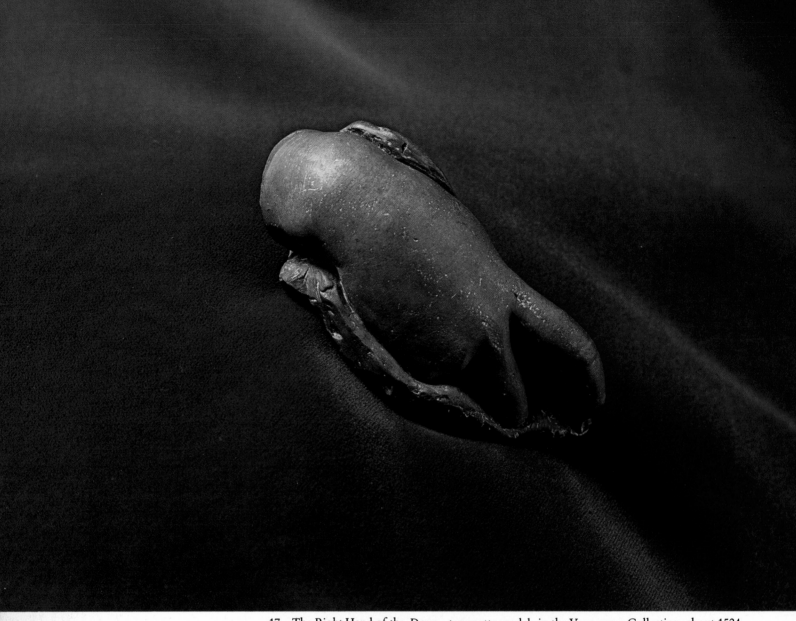

17 The Right Hand of the *Dawn*—terracotta model, in the Vancouver Collection, about 1524.

The right hand of the *Dawn*

Length 4-21/64in. 108mm.

In this terracotta model (Fig. 17) of a right hand with a piece of garment beneath, the graceful right hand (Fig. 18) of the marble sculpture of the "Dawn" can be identified. The model is now in the Collection in Vancouver.

The hand of the huge seven-foot marble statue (Fig. 19) conforms in fine detail to the delicate model (Fig. 20). Although the marble sculpture of the hand is considerably larger than that of the model, the proportions have been perfectly transposed by Michelangelo without losing any of the grace of the original model.

For drying and firing purposes, this clay sketch has had its interior hollowed out through its base by the Master. There also exists across the base a clay bridge for strengthening purposes.

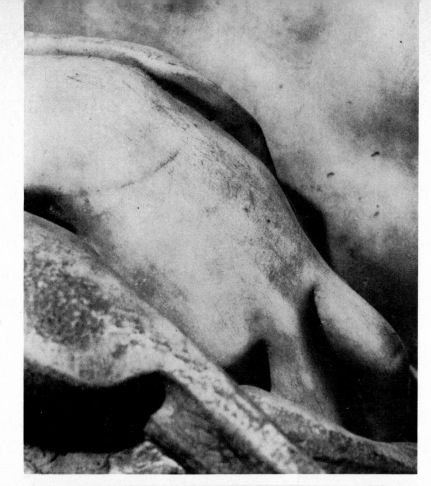

18
The Right Hand of the *Dawn*,
detail of the marble statue in the
Medici Chapel, Florence,
about 1524-1531.

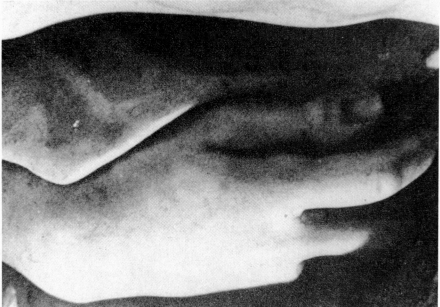

19
The Right Hand of the *Dawn*,
detail of the marble statue in the
Medici Chapel, Florence.

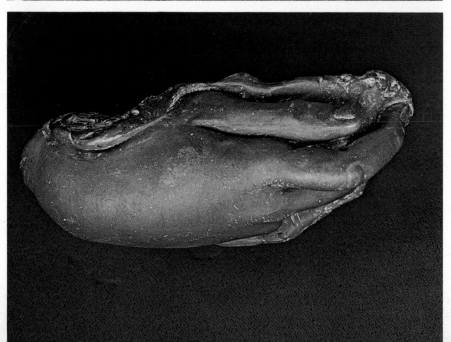

20
The Right Hand of the *Dawn*—
terracotta model, in the
Vancouver Collection.

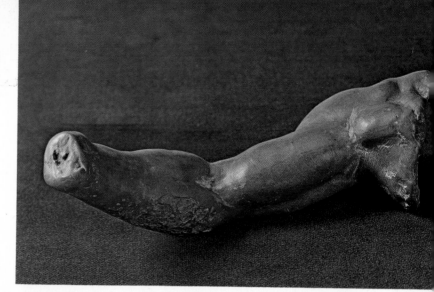

A right male arm

(the right arm of the *Evening*)

Length 8-1/16in. 204mm.

This model (Figs. 21 and 22), now
in the Canadian Collection, according to Henry Thode is very possibly
for the right arm of "Evening" in
the Medici Chapel, as it is very
similar to the statue, with the arm a
little more bent in the final sculpture (Figs. 23 and 24).

23
The Right Arm of the
Evening, detail of the marble
statue in the Medici Chapel,
Florence, about 1524-1531.

21   A Right Male Arm—
terracotta model, in the
Vancouver Collection,
about 1502. (*Opposite*).

24
The Right Arm of the
Evening, detail of the marble
statue in the Medici Chapel,
Florence.

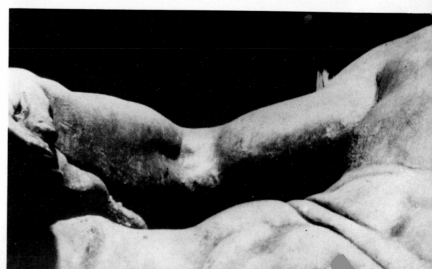

25 Engraving at Holkam Hall, England, after a copy of Michelangelo's lost cartoon for the *Battle of Cascina*, 1504-1505—British Museum, London.

According to Goldscheider, the model (Fig. 26) belongs to the period of the "Battle of Cascina" cartoon (Fig. 25) and arms of a similar character (Figs. 27 and 28) are to be seen in the "Slaves" of the Sistine Chapel ceiling fresco.

A *Slave* in the ceiling fresco of the
Sistine Chapel, Rome, 1508-1512.

26   A Right Male Arm—terracotta model,
in the Vancouver Collection.

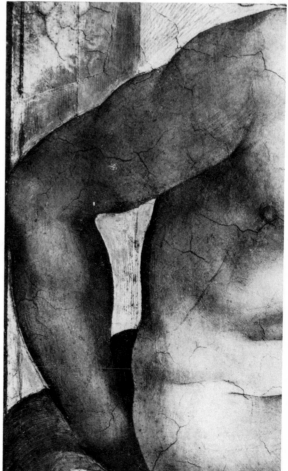

28   A Right Arm, detail of a *Slave* in the ceiling
fresco of the Sistine Chapel, Rome, 1508-1512.

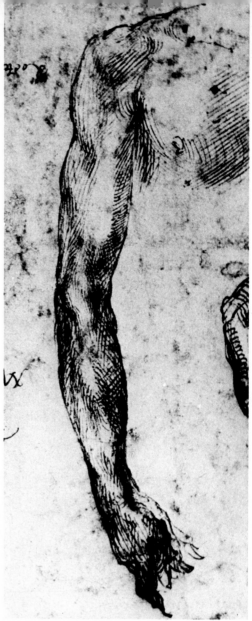

29 Studies by Michelangelo of a Torso and of a
Right Arm, in the Casa Buonarroti, about 1534.

30 A Study of a Right Arm by Michelangelo,
in the Louvre, 1501-1502.

Professor Goldscheider also states that this model in the
Vancouver Collection is simply a study by Michelangelo. There are
a number of drawings by the Master which show arms (Figs. 29
and 30) that have a close affinity to the clay model.

This original terracotta model by Michelangelo appears to have
been sliced into two parts prior to firing, or it may have been cast
from an original wax model, as the model's patina appears to be
slightly waxy and there is a very faint seam showing on part of the
model's surface. It has a rough and splintered appearance on the
underside of the forearm due to the firing process, combined with
the incomplete surface modelling shown in Figure 22, where the
underside of the forearm is intended to rest against the right thigh
of the figure. The model has been hollowed out at the upper part
of the shoulder, where scooping-out marks are clearly discernible;
otherwise it is solid throughout.

3
A Left Arm, Shoulder and Part of the Bac
—terracotta model, in the Vancouve
Collection, about 1524. (*Opposite*

48

A left arm, shoulder and part of the back

(left arm, shoulder and part of back of the *Evening*)

Length 10-3/4in. 273mm. Diagonal length 12-1/16in. 307mm.

This terracotta model (Figs. 31, 32 and 35) in the Vancouver Collection was used, according to Goldscheider and Thode, for the left arm, shoulder and part of the back of the statue "Evening" (Figs. 33 and 34). The model shows, however, that the bearing of the marble statue would originally have been planned somewhat differently.

Professor Goldscheider believes that the model was also used by Michelangelo for the left arm and shoulder of "Night" in the Medici Chapel, as can be seen in a comparison with his drawing for the alteration of the left arm of "Night" (Fig. 37) in the British

32 A Left Arm, Shoulder and Part of the Back—terracotta model, in the Vancouver Collection.

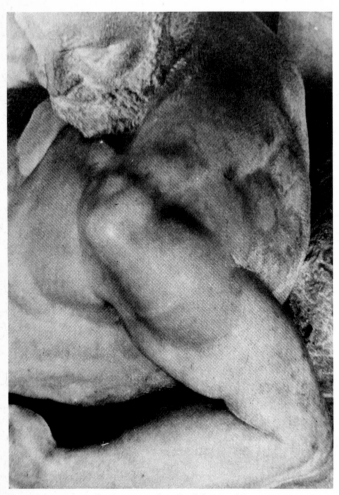

33 The *Evening*, detail of the marble statue in the Medici Chapel, Florence, about 1524-1531.

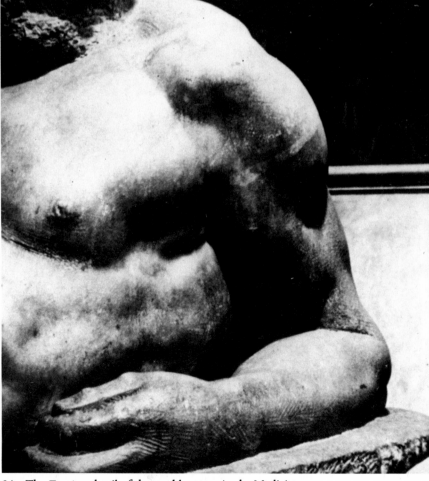

34 The *Evening*, detail of the marble statue in the Medici Chapel, Florence, about 1524-1531.

Museum. The model, according to Goldscheider, was again used for a "River God" and he further states that it must have been famous when it belonged to the von Praun Collection in Bologna, in about the year 1590, as it was used by Giovanni Battista Paggi for his painting "Venus and Cupid" (Fig. 36).

The beautifully sculptured model of a "Left Shoulder and Part of the Back" (Fig. 31) is certainly one of the finest of Michelangelo's initial and inspirational creations in clay. As an original clay model it has been hollowed out at the back, with scooping-out marks clearly visible. The arm of the model is solid throughout.

35 A Left Arm, Shoulder and Part of the Back — terracotta model, in the Vancouver Collection.

36 *Venus and Cupid*, detail from the painting by Giovanni Battista Paggi (1554-1627) in the Palazzo Bianco, Genoa.

37 Drawing for the Alteration of the Left Arm of the *Night*, by Michelangelo, in the British Museum, 1526-1530.

The *Day* Height 7in. 178mm.; Length 12½ in. 318mm.

38   The *Day*—terracotta model, in the Museum of Fine Arts, Houston, Texas, about 1524.

This model (Fig. 38) of the "Day" in the Medici Chapel, is now in the Museum of Fine Arts, Houston, Texas. The right foot of the model is missing. The garment is indicated in its entirety beneath the figurine, but not in the final sculpture (Fig. 39). The back muscles are simplified in the statue, whereas they are more pronounced and intricate in the model (Fig. 40). Other muscles show a greater fullness in the model.

What is of particular importance in this wonderful small sculpture is its finished head and fully defined face. The model (Fig. 43) shows us how Michelangelo intended the

39 The *Day*—marble statue in the Medici Chapel, Florence, about 1524-1531.

40

The *Day*—terracotta model, in the Museum of Fine Arts, Houston, Texas.

42 The Head of the *Vanquished*, detail of the marble statue, *Victory* in the Palazzo Vecchio, Florence, 1525-1530.

head and face to appear, yet in the marble (Fig. 41) the head was left unfinished and sculptured in only very rough form. The shape of the head in the model (Figs. 40 and 43), with its thick, curled hair set like a cap, its full beard framing an energetic face with a broad-set nose between painful and threatening eyes, corresponds almost perfectly with the head of the "Vanquished" (Fig. 42) which was also created by Michelangelo at about the same time. The differences between the clay model and the marble sculpture, especially those relating to the completed head and face of the model, offer proof that the work in clay is older than the incomplete figure in the Medici Chapel.

According to the biographer Ridolfi, Tintoretto painted a portrait of himself holding a model of the "Evening". This self-portrait, which was actually an indirect tribute to Michelangelo by the Venetian painter, is now lost.

Tintoretto studied Michelangelo diligently, and as in the case of many other artists including Rubens (1577-1640), he fell under the spell of the four "Phases of the Day" in the Medici Chapel. He reproduced "Evening" and "Dawn" in his frescoes in the Palazzo Grimani Gussoni, which are known to us only through engravings by Zanetti, who also saw and recorded a number of lost drawings by Tintoretto after Michelangelo's sculpture.

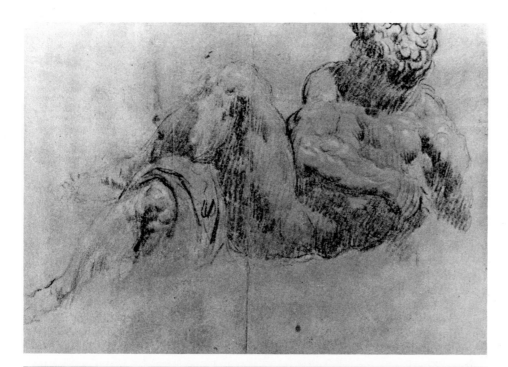

44 A Study after Michelangelo's *Day*, by Japoco Tintoretto, made from a preparatory model for the figure in the Medici Chapel. Charcoal on light blue paper, 13½ins. by 20ins. in the Metropolitan Museum of Art in New York City. The same figure is drawn on the reverse side of the paper.

45 The *Day*, a view of the back of the marble statue in the Medici Chapel, Florence.

Figure 44 shows a charcoal drawing by Tintoretto, on light blue-green paper, of the figure of the "Day" but it differs considerably from the marble sculpture reclining on the tomb of Giuliano. The drawing shows the back of the "Day", which in the marble by Michelangelo (Fig. 45) is towards the wall of the Chapel and is executed only in an incomplete and rough outline, as is the case in a number of his masterpieces.

46 An additional view of the back of
the marble statue of the *Day*.

The treatment in stone of the unfinished left arm and shoulder, as well as the uncarved right hand and parts of the torso of the marble figure of the "Day" by Michelangelo (Fig. 46), when compared to the other more finished figures in the Tomb, leads us to believe that it was one of the last sculptures that the Great Master made before abandoning the Medici project in 1534.

Tintoretto's drawing (Fig. 44) of the "Day" shows a complete figure, and not the incomplete back of the stone sculpture by Michelangelo, and it is therefore evident that he did not do a direct drawing of the back of the marble statue. Moreover, in order to do so, it would have required the difficult task of moving the statue, as its back is set high and directly against the Medici Chapel wall. In fact, it is doubtful that Tintoretto ever visited the Chapel, as there is no historical reference to the event. Figure 47, which shows the back of the terracotta model of the "Day", illustrates the strong possibility that Tintoretto did his drawing from the clay model of the "Day", which is now in the museum in Houston. As this model (Fig. 48) shows at its back a far more completely sculptured figure, especially with regard to the left arm and shoulder, as well as the right hand and parts of the torso, there exists, therefore, yet another proof that the model was created prior to the incomplete marble sculpture. The back of the model shows three comparatively large holes which were used in the scooping-out of its hol-

47 The *Day*, a view from above
of the terracotta model in the
Museum of Fine Arts,
Houston, Texas.

48 The *Day*, the back of the terracotta model in the
Museum of Fine Arts, Houston, Texas.

56

low interior, and for firing purposes. It is obvious that the model was not formed in a mould; if such had been the case the three holes would have no purpose.

In a drawing (Fig. 49) by Tintoretto, in the Louvre, the figure of the "Day" is shown from the back, from slightly above and at a slant. The left shoulder pointing towards the viewer is a mass of foreshortened limbs and it is much more complete, as it is in the terracotta model, than in the sculptured marble figure of the "Day" (Fig. 45). On the reverse of the sheet the same figure is shown at the same angle, but drawn with the paper held vertically, thus allowing room to draw only the towering back muscles which, like the clay model now in Houston, are most intricate and pronounced.

49   A Study after Michelangelo's *Day*, by Jacopo Tintoretto (in the Louvre), made from a preparatory model for the figure in the Medici Chapel. The same figure is drawn on the reverse side of the paper.

Ridolfi, in his biography of Tintoretto, described the care with which the artist "...drew bodies from life, placing them in various attitudes...recording their infinite foreshortenings". Tintoretto was fond of suspending (with threads inserted through small holes) wax and clay models from the roof-beams of his studio so that he could study their forms from below, and in order to better ascertain the foreshortenings required for figures to be painted on ceilings.

Ridolfi also mentions that this great Venetian painter moulded with extreme care small models of figures as a means of determining the effects of light and shade in their design. As in the case of Michelangelo, he often modelled his small wax and clay sculptures from the cadaver—he attended anatomy schools—and imparted to them a far more complete character than was the custom of other artists who also used models. In some cases Tintoretto suspended models in a wooden or paper box by means of a string or thread tied to a small hole in the model. Having also made an aperture in the box in order to admit the light of a candle, he was able to study postures which would have been very difficult, if not impossible, to obtain from the living model.

Starting in his student days, Tintoretto collected throughout his lifetime fragments of antique sculpture, casts and bas-reliefs. He used as studies a large number of Michelangelo models, some of which were very likely originals and others undoubtedly copies. He is known to have owned an original Michelangelo clay model of "Hercules and Cacus", and also models for the four "Phases of the Day" ("Allegories") in the Medici Chapel.

Vasari, in his "Lives of the Artists", states that when Daniele da Volterra (1509-1566) was in Florence he made plaster casts of almost all of the marble figures by Michelangelo in the Medici Chapel. These copies, now lost, must have been very similar to the over-life-size stucco copy made of the "Day" by Vincenzo Danti in 1573, which is now in the Accademia in Perugia. A number of art historians have rightly (or perhaps wrongly) stated that Volterra also made at the same time small clay models of the Medici Tomb figures, and have tried rather unsuccessfully to directly connect these now lost small clay models with the models of the "Allegories" which are known to have been in the possession of Tintoretto and used by him in some of his drawings. Charles de Tolnay, on p. 155 of *The Medici Chapel* states that the drawings by Tintoretto after the "Allegories" and "Duke Guiliano" were at least partly made after models by Daniele da Volterra, and on p. 156 of the same volume he says that copies by Volterra after the figures in the Medici Chapel were acquired by Tintoretto and used by him for purposes of study. As one of the references to the foregoing, de Tolnay quotes Ridolfi (*Le Maraviglie dell'arte,* Venice, 1648, II, pp. 13f), who in any case believed that Tintoretto possessed original small models by Michelangelo.

As previously stated, there is a strong possibility that the clay model of the "Day" which was formerly in the von Praun Collection was the actual Michelangelo model which Tintoretto used for the two drawings shown in Figures 44 and 49, and which he must have turned over many times while he explored its complicated movements as an exercise in form and foreshortening. The clay models of the "Day", the "Night", the "Dawn" and the "Evening" which were formerly in the Praunsche Kabinett may very well have come from Tintoretto's studio. At the time of Tintoretto's death Paul von Praun was age 46, and had been acquiring art in Italy for many years, in fact the von Praun Collection contained two very fine paintings by Tintoretto and five of his drawings, as well as a number of engravings of his works. It is of interest to note that de Tolnay on p. 142 of his *The Medici Chapel* is of the opinion that four drawings by Tintoretto in Christ Church College, Oxford, were made by him after a now lost small model of Giuliano de' Medici, which he says was probably a copy of the original model by Michelangelo. On this premise alone it then could also be said that Daniele da Volterra's now lost small models of the "Allegories" (assuming that they at one time did exist, and ignoring the question as to whether or not they were ever in the possession of Tintoretto) were probably copies of original small models by Michelangelo, namely the four "Allegories" in the von Praun Collection.

A drawing (Fig. 50) by El Greco, formerly in the Vasari Collection and now in the Munich Print Room, has heretofore been considered to be a sketch of a lost model by Michelangelo for the "Day". The model in the drawing is almost identical to the clay model of the "Day" in the von Praun Collection, with the exception that the left leg in the drawing does not cross the right thigh of the figure. This, however, can perhaps be put down to artistic licence. The

50 A Drawing after Michelangelo's *Day*, by El Greco, made from a preparatory model for the figure in the Medici Chapel. Black and white chalk on blue paper, 23½ins. by 13½ins. in the Munich Print Room, about 1568.

51 The *Day,* a view from directly above of the marble statue in the Medici Chapel, Florence.

model shown in the drawing is very different from the final version in stone (Fig. 51). It was sketched by the young El Greco during his stay in Venice, very likely in Tintoretto's studio.

Forming a part of Carl von Lützow's article in 1876 on the Haehnel Collection ("Die Michelangelo-Ausstellung in Florenz") are fairly early examples of photography. Photographs of the Haehnel Collection which are shown are of those models for the "Day", the "Night" and the "Dawn", as well as a model for "A Left Arm, Shoulder and Part of the

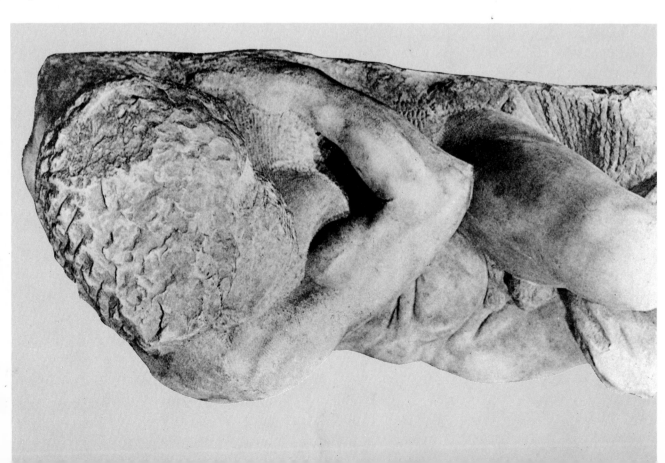

Back" (see Fig. 31). It is apparent that the breakage and subsequent loss of the left foot of the terracotta model of the "Day" must have occurred after 1876, and that the damage to the toes of the model's right foot must also have taken place after that time, as von Lützow's photograph of a plaster cast reproduction (displaying many obvious seams) of the original terracotta model shows these parts to be attaching and that the model is complete in every respect. Prints also available to Lützow of the actual terracotta models of the "Day" and of the "Night" were unsuitable for reproduction.

Figure 52 is an illustration of a replica in bronze of the terracotta model of the "Day" which is now in the Houston Museum, with the exception that the above-noted former appendages to the clay model are no longer part of it. They are part of the bronze casting, however, as in the 1876 illustration of the reproduction by von Lützow. The added base of the reproduction appears also to be identical to the base in the bronze casting. The bronze is very possibly a cast of the copy photographed by Lützow, done in the middle of the nineteenth century while the original terracotta model was in Haehnel's possession (Haehnel is famous throughout Germany for his sculpture in bronze) and it may even have been made at a much earlier date. The bronze casting is of particular importance because it shows the completeness of the clay model before the loss of the left foot and the damage to the toes of the right foot.

52 A bronze 12½in. cast of the terracotta model of the *Day* in the Museum of Fine Arts, Houston, Texas. In the possession of Edward Halprin, Vancouver, Canada, about 1850.

61

The left foot of the *Day*

Height 3in. 77mm.;
Length 5in. 128mm.

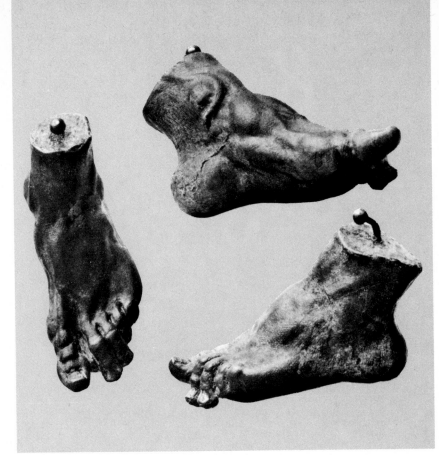

53   The Left Foot of the *Day*—terracotta model, whereabouts unknown, about 1524.

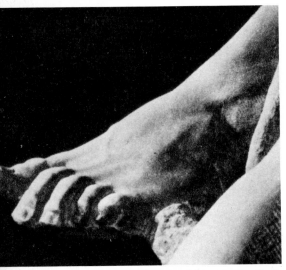

54   The Left Foot of the *Day*, detail of the marble statue in the Medici Chapel, Florence, about 1524-1531.

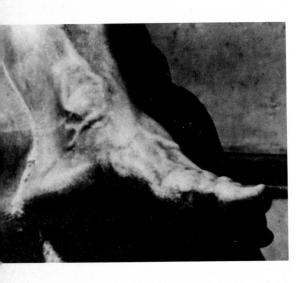

The present location of this completely executed model (Fig. 53) of the left foot of the marble statue of the "Day" (Figs. 54 and 55) is not known. It is possible that von Praun bought the model from Alessandro Vittorio, a former favourite student of Michelangelo.

Henry Thode has stated:

"Not without interest is the note published by Cicogna, that Grimm noted, according to which in 1562 Alessandro Vittorio acquired Michelangelo's model for the left foot of the 'Day' directly from a Bologna art dealer, and it seems very unlikely that this famous sculptor should have bought a falsification. And in this way the presumption may be allowed at least that this piece comes perhaps from this same possession as Praun's objects."

55   The Left Foot of the *Day*, detail of the marble statue in the Medici Chapel, Florence.

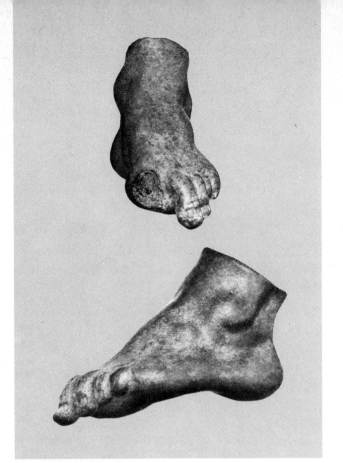

A left foot
(the left foot of the *Night*?)

Height 2in. 51mm.; Length 4in. 102mm.

The whereabouts of this clay model (Fig. 56) of a left foot, with a missing big toe, is not known. There appears to be a remarkable similarity between this model and the left foot of the marble sculpture "Night", as shown in Figure 61. Henry Thode was in doubt that this small terracotta was actually by the hand of Michelangelo.

56   A Left Foot—terracotta model, whereabouts unknown, about 1524.

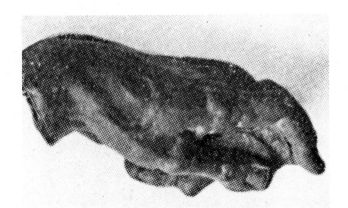

57   The Left Hand of the *Day*—terracotta model, whereabouts unknown, about 1524.

The left hand of the *Day*

Length 3in. 77mm.

The present location of the small clay model (Fig. 57) with the garment beneath, of the left hand (Fig. 58) of the marble statue "Day" in the Medici Chapel, is not known.

58
The Left Hand of the *Day*, detail of the marble statue in the Medici Chapel, Florence, about 1524-1531.

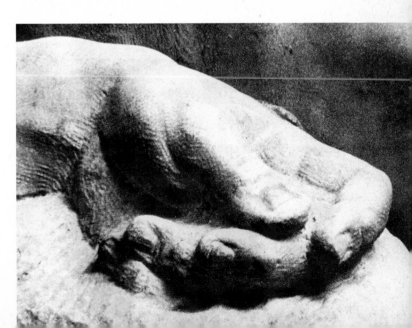

The *Night* Height 8½ in. 217mm.; Length 10½ in. 267mm.

59   The *Night*— terracotta model, in the Victoria and Albert Museum, London, about 1524.

The model of the "Night" (Fig. 59) which is now in the Victoria and Albert Museum, has body mouldings of the same anatomic perfection as the two other "Phases of the Day" which were also formerly in the Haehnel-von Praun Collection, namely the "Dawn" and the "Day".

The back of the model was damaged during the firing process. The lower right arm and the right foot are missing on the model, and slight damage and isolated cracks appear on it. The head of the model is somewhat damaged, most noticeably at the bridge of the nose, and was at one time broken off. The model appears to have been rather badly mended in plaster in the areas of the neck, the left eye, temple and cheek. The head of the model (Fig. 60) shows, however, a higher sense of beauty, especially with regard to the softer lines of the eyes, of the nostrils and of the mouth, than is shown in the female form executed in stone (Fig. 61) in the Medici Chapel.

Figure 62 shows three sketches by Rubens of the rather muscular figure of the "Night", from the side and from the

60 The *Night*—terracotta model, in the Victoria and Albert Museum, London.

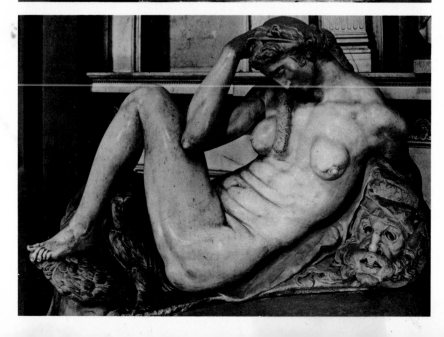

61
The *Night*, marble statue in the Medici Chapel, Florence, about 1524-1531.

62 Three Studies after Michelangelo's *Night*, by Peter Paul Rubens (Lugt Collection, The Hague), made from a preparatory model for the figure in the Medici Chapel.

63 (*Top right*) The *Night*—terracotta model, in the Victoria and Albert Museum, London.

back. To enable Rubens to make a direct drawing of the back of the marble figure of the "Night"—two of the sketches show different views of the back of the "Night"—would have necessitated the difficult job of moving the statue, which is set high with its back against the wall of the Medici Chapel, and it is very doubtful that the large stone sculpture was moved to accommodate Rubens. The fact that these sketches show the completed left hand of the "Night" in three positions is further proof that the marble sculpture in the Chapel, with its left hand a shapeless lump (Fig. 66), could not have been the subject copied by Rubens, and that he must have drawn these three sketches from a model made by Michelangelo preparatory to the final stone sculpture. There is every reason to believe that the terracotta model of the "Night" from the von Praun Collection, which shows a left hand exactly as in the sketches and with the top of the drapery folded in the same manner over the end of the extended index finger, was the model copied by Rubens.

The position of the extremely clever and very lively-looking "Mask" in the model (Fig. 63) is a little more turned to the right than in the marble, and it is also somewhat different, as is the left hand of "Night", which is shown in completed form above the forehead of the "Mask" in the model, but as a damaged and incomplete piece of sculpture in the marble statue (Fig. 66).

The garment under the body of the model of the "Night" is more folded than it is in the stone statue, and it is obvious that Michelangelo has done a more finished and realistic job with respect to the "Owl" in the marble than in the one in clay. There are also differences in the poppy leaves under the left foot, and in the base under the bunch of poppies, which is in the form of a cushion and does not have in the model the beautifully rounded and draped garment pleats of the marble statue.

Figure 64 shows the back of the marble sculpture of the "Night" and Figure 65 shows the back of the clay model of the same subject. On the back of the model there appears

66

the extensive damage mentioned in the Murr Catalogue and this is undoubtedly the result of the firing process. There are still portions of the skin surface of the model at the back part of the right shoulder which show us the characteristic muscular structure of Michelangelo's sculptural style. There exists no left arm and elbow at the back of the stone figure of the "Night". In fact, only the uncut portion of the marble is seen where the arm and elbow should be. The terracotta model, however, shows at its back a carefully executed left arm and elbow which from all angles is anatomically perfect. It is apparent that the back of the model, which also includes the top part of the bag of poppies draped over its right thigh, shows a more completely sculptured form than the one in marble, and that many parts of the statue's back did not progress beyond the first rough indications. As in the case of the statue of "Dawn", the fact that the back of the marble statue of the "Night" was left partly incomplete by Michelangelo is of no significance, as both these figures are set high and close to the wall of the Medici Chapel, so that only the front of these figures can be seen. It is significant, however, that their backs would be unavailable to a copyist, even in the very unlikely event that he were allowed to enter the Chapel for the purpose of copying in clay the marble sculptures by Michelangelo.

Meier-Graefe in his 1924 publication on the Haehnel Collection points out, with reference to the model of the "Night", one almost insignificant but highly important detail; that the big toe of the left foot of the finished marble statue appears to be striving upwards, whereas in the clay model it is in a more normal position.

The many differences that exist between the model of the "Night" and the final marble figure prove that the clay model is not a copy of the marble sculpture, but rather that the Medici Chapel work is a copy in slightly altered and unfinished form of the previous beautifully complete sculptured model in clay.

64 (*Top left*) The *Night*, the back of the marble statue in the Medici Chapel, Florence.

65 The *Night*, the back of the terracotta model in the Victoria and Albert Museum, London.

66 The Mask of the *Night*, detail of the marble statue in the Medici Chapel, Florence.

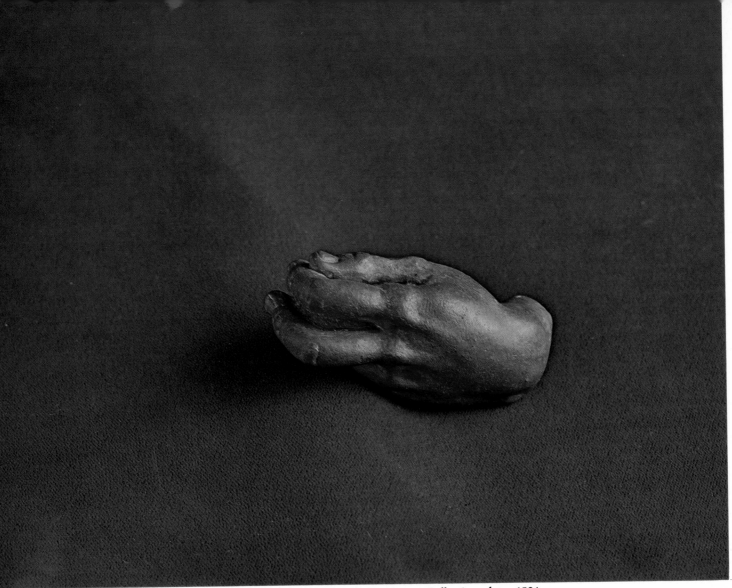

67   The Left Hand of the *Night*—terracotta model in the Vancouver Collection, about 1524.

68   The Left Hand of the *Night*,
detail of the marble statue in the
Medici Chapel, Florence, about 1524.

The left hand of the *Night*

Length 3-3/32in. 78mm.

This beautiful study (Fig. 67) in terracotta for the left hand of "Night", was not completed in the marble sculpture in the Medici Chapel statue. In the statue Michelangelo has made the forearm too short and the hand, above the brow of the "Mask" (Fig. 68), has been left by him a shapeless lump of stone. The differences speak for the genuineness of the model.

This clay model, which in its elegance corresponds very closely to the model for the right hand of "Dawn" (Fig. 17), is now in the Collection in Vancouver. It is an original clay model, made solid throughout and then fired as such.

68

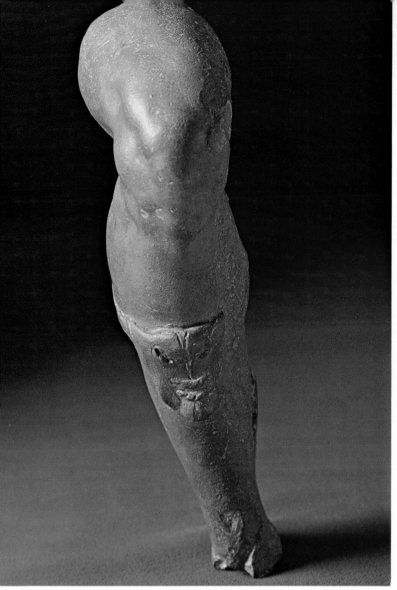

69 The Right Bent Leg of *Giuliano de'Medici*—terracotta model, in the Vancouver Collection, about 1524.

70 The Right Bent Leg of *Giuliano de'Medici*, detail of the marble statue in the Medici Chapel, Florence, about 1524-1531.

The right bent leg of *Giuliano de'Medici*

Height 6-13/16in. 173mm.

This clay model (Fig. 69) of the lower thigh, right bent knee and leg of "Giuliano de' Medici", Duke of Nemours, is now in the Vancouver Collection. The inner side of the leg is somewhat splintered off and demonstrates the fact that Michelangelo often left portions of the surfaces of his models incomplete, especially where they were not to be seen by the eventual viewers of the finished marble (Fig. 70).

In the model the overhang of the stocking shows small differences as against the statue. It is narrower and longer than in the marble and the model does not have such a distinctly marked crimp at the top of the stocking's overhang. The model bears the clear sign of genius and the little differences show clearly that the model is not an imitation of the marble.

This original clay model was made solid throughout and then fired as such. The splintered and chipped appearance on the inner side of the model is very possibly due to the incomplete modelling combined with the effects of the firing process.

71 A Right Bent Leg—
terracotta model, in the
Vancouver Collection,
about 1514.

A right bent leg

The right bent leg of *Giuliano de'Medici.*

Height 5-5/16in. 135mm.

Henry Thode stated that this model (Fig. 71) of a right bent leg now in the Canadian Collection, could be a first general study for the right leg (Fig. 70) of the marble statue of "Giuliano de'Medici", Duke of Nemours, in the Medici Chapel.

The model (Fig. 74) could also have been used as the preliminary study for the right bent leg of the "Heroic Captive" (Fig. 72) in the Louvre, or for the right bent leg of Apollo (Fig. 73) in the Museo Nazionale del Bargello, Florence.

This hollow model was originally made solid, with interior clay later scooped out through the openings in its extremities, in preparation for the firing.

The Right Leg of the *Apollo*, detail of the marble statue in the Museo Nazionale del Bargello, Florence, about 1530.

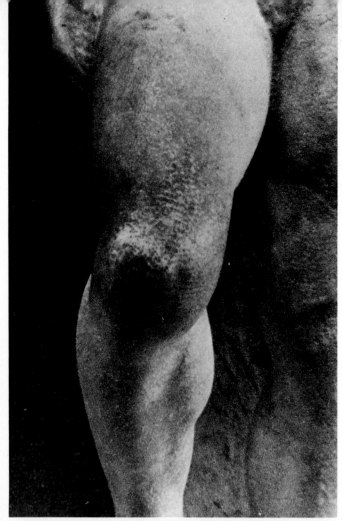

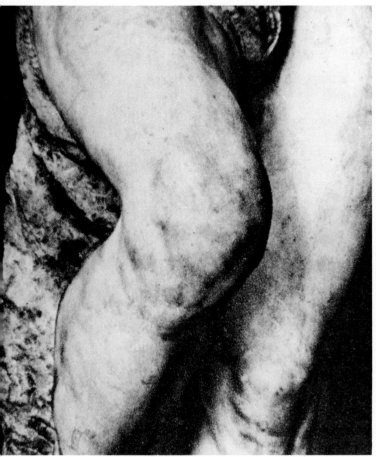

72   The Right Leg of the *Heroic Captive,* detail of the marble statue in the Louvre, Paris, 1514-1516.

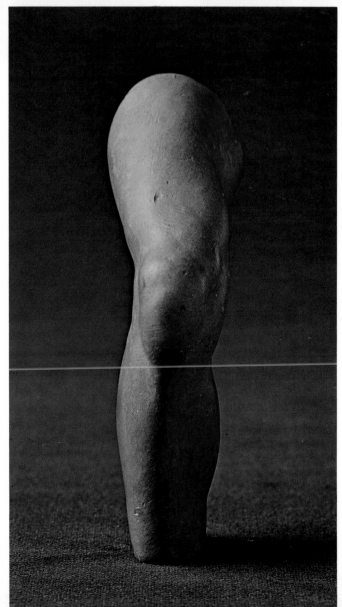

74
A Right Bent Leg—terracotta model, in the Vancouver Collection.

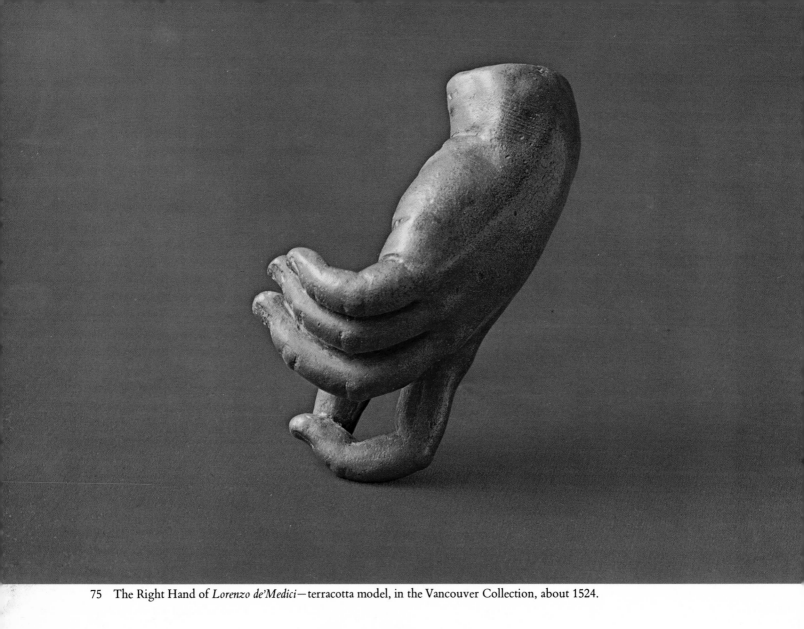

75 The Right Hand of *Lorenzo de'Medici*—terracotta model, in the Vancouver Collection, about 1524.

The right hand of
Lorenzo de'Medici

Length 4-13/16in. 122mm.

In this terracotta (Fig. 75) by Michelangelo in the Vancouver Collection, can be seen an example of the importance of such studies to the Master, and it provides us with a deeper understanding of his work methods. This model for the marble right hand (Fig. 77) of "Lorenzo de'Medici", Duke of Urbino, (Fig. 76) in the Medici Chapel, shows the manner in which such scrupulous preparatory works were used.

The model, alongside that of the subsequently executed hand in marble, is illustrated in Ludwig Goldscheider's *A Survey of Michelangelo's Models in Wax and Clay* on a full two-page comparative basis.

76 *Lorenzo de'Medici*, marble statue in the Medici Chapel, Florence, about 1524-1531.

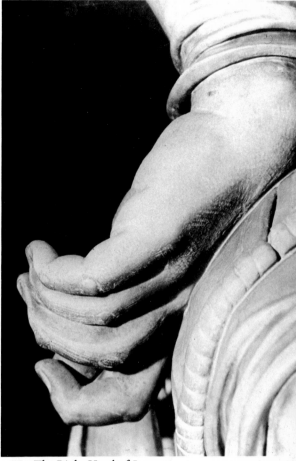

77 The Right Hand of *Lorenzo de'Medici*, detail of the marble statue in the Medici Chapel, Florence.

73

78 Mirror image of the Right Hand of *Lorenzo de'Medici*—terracotta model in the Vancouver Collection.

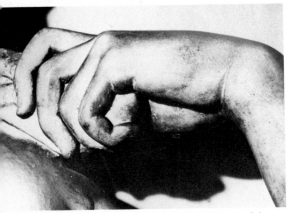

79 The Left Hand of the *Dawn,* detail of the marble statue in the Medici Chapel, Florence, about 1524-1531.

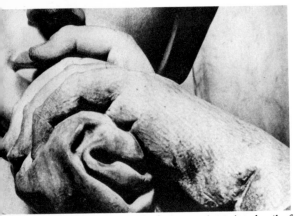

80 The Left Hand of *Lorenzo de'Medici,* detail of the marble statue in the Medici Chapel, Florence, about 1524-1531.

81 The Left Hand of *Isaiah,* detail of *Isaiah,* in the ceiling fresco of the Sistine Chapel, Rome, 1508-1512.

74

When the image of this wonderful work is reversed (Fig. 78), one can recognize the left hand of the "Dawn" (Fig. 79) and the left hand of "Lorenzo de'Medici" (Fig. 80), as well as the left hand of "Isaiah" (Fig. 81) in the Sistine Chapel ceiling fresco.

The inner side of the clay hand (Fig. 82) is splintered due to the firing and to the incomplete modelling of its surface. This part of the model is turned away from the viewer as it rests against Lorenzo's right thigh and it cannot be seen in the marble sculpture. Of interest is the incised cutting around the fingernails of the model, and the raised folds of the knuckles. This is characteristic of most of the finished hands in Michelangelo's sculpture and paintings, as can be seen in the right hand of "Giuliano de'Medici" (Fig. 83) and in the left hand of "Isaiah" (Fig. 81).

As with all the models in the Haehnel-von Praun Collection, this clay model is of terracotta, with the clay of its hollow interior having been scooped out through an opening in the middle of the wrist. Scooping-out marks can be clearly discerned in the hollow interior.

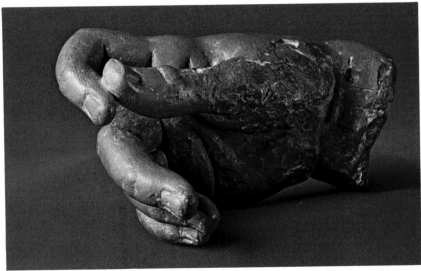

82 The Right Hand of *Lorenzo de'Medici*—terracotta model, in the Vancouver Collection.

83 The Right Hand of *Giuliano de'Medici,* detail of the marble statue in the Medici Chapel, Florence, about 1524-1531.

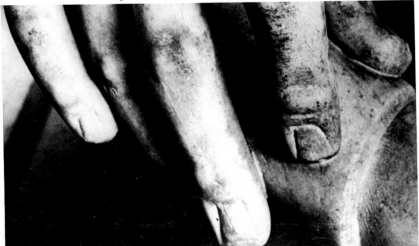

84 The Left Hand of *Giuliano de'Medici* — terracotta model, whereabouts unknown, about 1524.

The left hand of *Giuliano de'Medici*

Length 4in. 102mm.

The present whereabouts of the small model of the left hand of "Giuliano de'Medici" (Fig. 84) is not known. According to Thode, who failed to photograph the model, the completely different position of the baton held by the left hand (Fig. 85) in the marble statue of "Giuliano de'Medici", Duke of Nemours, in the Medici Chapel, as compared to the clay model, seems to disprove a positive relationship between the model and the statue. The baton held by the left hand in the marble is clearly defined, but not so with respect to the clay model wherein, according to Thode, the hand seems to be holding something rather of a soft nature. Henry Thode has stated, however, that the model shows without a doubt the authority of Michelangelo, and writes:

"The similarity in motive is so great that we can assume it to be a first draft of the hand which later shows a changed concept with the extended middle finger and in a different position. It is with regard thereto that this model, so similar in its language of forms and its execution, deserves special consideration and does not leave any doubt of its creation by Michelangelo."

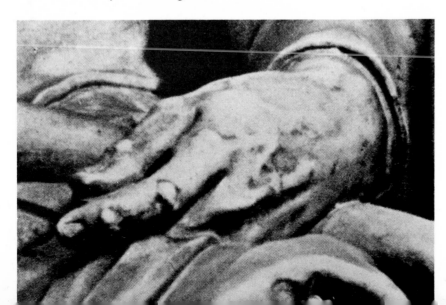

85 The Left Hand of *Giuliano de'Medici*, detail of the marble statue in the Medici Chapel, Florence, about 1524-1531.

The back side and left thigh of a reclining figure

Length 10-3/4in. 273mm.
Diagonal length 12-1/16in. 307mm.

The fact that single parts of the body were a special
peculiarity of Michelangelo's form study is well
demonstrated by a clay model by the Master of a
back side and left thigh of a reclining figure (Fig.
88). This particularly fine terracotta model, which
is now in the Vancouver Collection, shows a perfect knowledge of the human anatomy, and was
used, according to Ludwig Goldscheider, as a study
for the left thigh of the "Night" (Fig. 86) in the
Medici Chapel, as well as for the back view of the
"Dawn" (Fig. 87), and for Michelangelo's lost
"Leda" painting (Fig. 90). The model (Fig. 89) was
also used as a study for the left thigh of the reclining marble figure (Fig. 91) of the "Evening" in the
Medici Chapel.

86   The *Night*, detail of the marble statue in the Medici
Chapel, Florence, about 1524-1531.

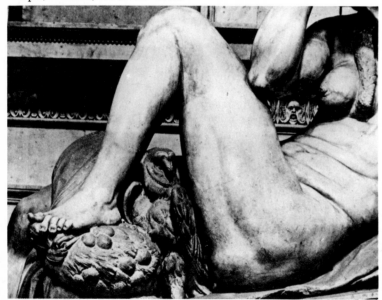

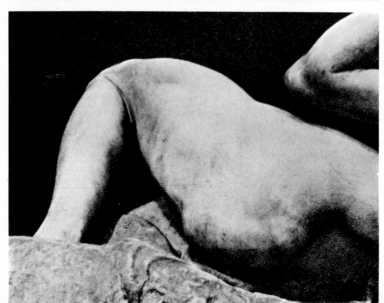

87   The *Dawn*, detail (back view) of the marble statue in
the Medici Chapel, Florence, about 1524-1531.

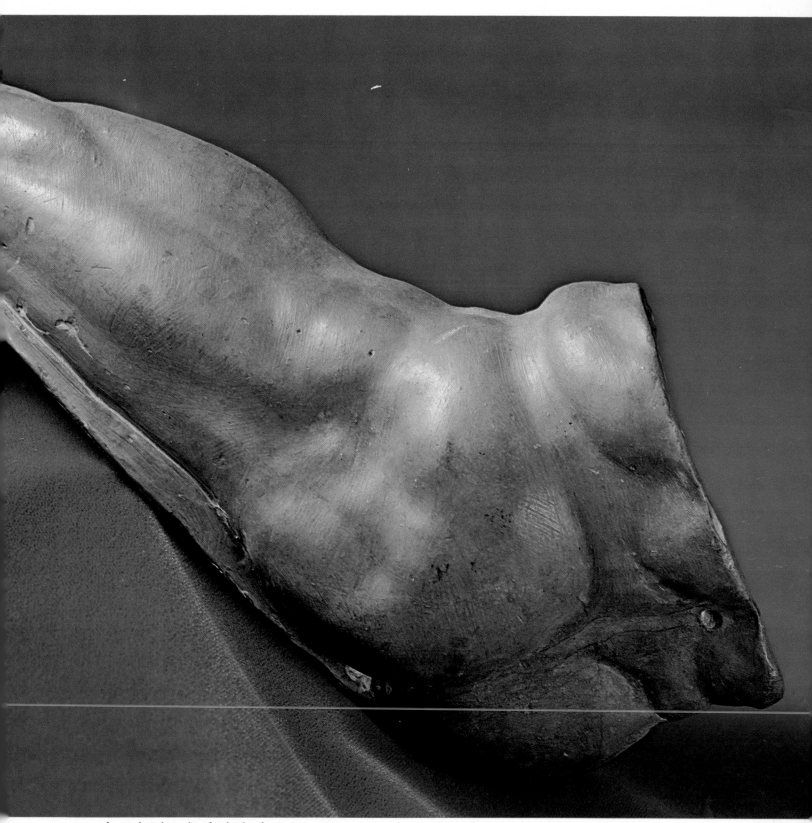

88   The Back Side and Left Thigh of a Reclining Figure—terracotta model, in the Vancouver Collection, about 1524.

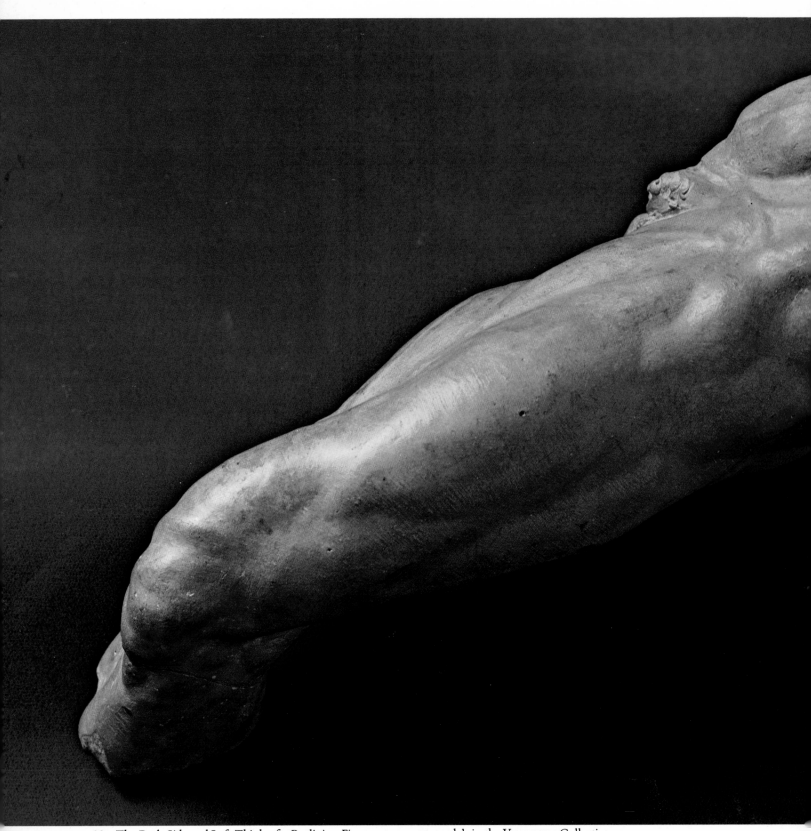

89   The Back Side and Left Thigh of a Reclining Figure—terracotta model, in the Vancouver Collection.

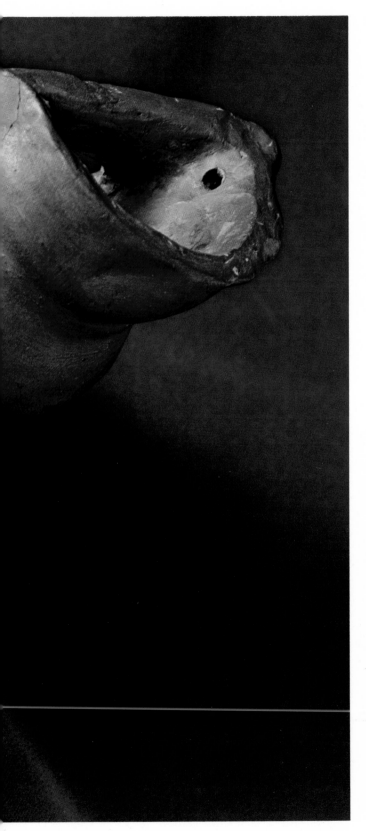

90 A Study for the *Leda*, by Michelangelo, in the British Museum, London, 1530.

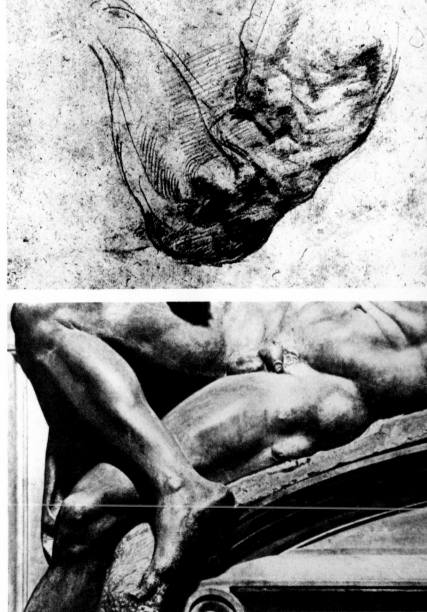

91 The *Evening*, detail of the marble statue in the Medici Chapel, Florence, about 1524-1531.

There is also a remarkable similarity between the model (Fig. 92) and the left thigh of "Laocoön" (Fig. 93) of the Roman copy of the "Laocoön Group" in the Vatican Museum in Rome. The antique statue made a tremendous impression on Michelangelo, who had been asked by Pope Clement to restore the missing right arm of "Laocoön", but declined to do so in favour of Montorsoli. Thode stated that the model was undoubtedly a copy of the "Antique", but he did not know which one. The model should also be compared to the left thigh of the lost model "Samson Slaying the Philistines" by Michelangelo, in the "Self Portrait" by Gerard Dou, 1647, in the Dresden Picture Gallery.

The photograph of the model in Henry Thode's article on the Haehnel Collection shows the model to be complete with no breakage crack beneath the knee. Meier-Graefe, however, illustrates a small part of the model beneath the knee as a separate part. It can be assumed, therefore, that the breakage must have taken place between 1913 and 1924. In this original clay model the interior scoopings are clearly distinguishable. The model was not cut for hollowing-out purposes, as this was done through four openings in its base and back. The clay figure also has a small round hole in its upper back portion, possibly for suspension purposes.

92   The Back Side and Left Thigh of a Reclining Figure—terracotta model in the Vancouver Collection.

93
The Left Thigh of *Laocoön*, of the Roman copy in marble of the *Laocoön Group*, in the Vatican Museum, Rome, about 50 B.C.

There are a number of drawings (Figs. 94 to 96) by Michelangelo which can be related to the model. The study (Fig. 94) for a recumbent statue in the Medici Chapel, was drawn by Michelangelo after a male model, as he usually did for all his figures, male or female. Figure 95 should be compared with Figure 167 and the relationship noted between the drawing, the model and the painting. This comparison again demonstrates the use by Michelangelo of a model for many purposes and in various poses.

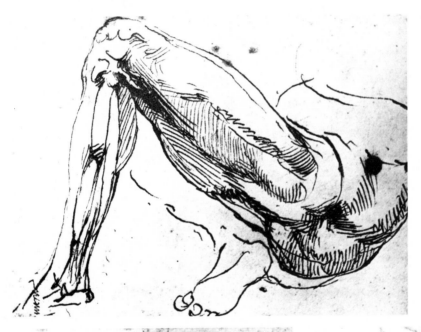

94 A Leg and Torso Study for a Recumbent Statue in the Medici Chapel, Florence, by Michelangelo, in the Casa Buonarroti, about 1525-1530.

95 (*Bottom left*)
Studies for *Haman* in a corner spandrel (Esther and Haman, 1511) of the Sistine Chapel Ceiling, Rome. Drawing by Michelangelo in the British Museum, London.

96
A Study of a Fallen Angel for the *Last Judgment*, by Michelangelo, in the British Museum, about 1536-1541.

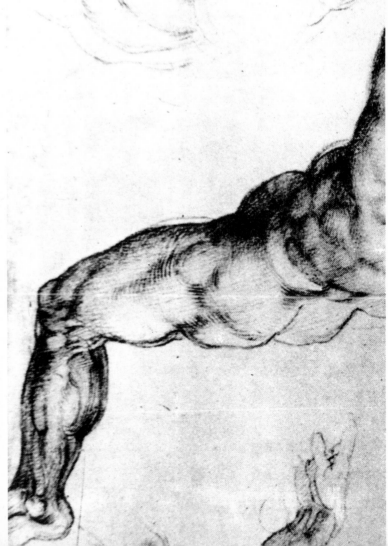

97
The *Medici Madonna*—terracotta
model now destroyed, formerly
in the Kaiser Friedrich Museum
(Staatliche Museum), Berlin,
about 1521.

The *Medici Madonna*

Height 9½ in. 242mm.

The Medici Chapel in Florence contains a 7½ foot high roughly-hewn marble statue of the Virgin suckling the child Jesus, as he straddles her left knee and turns to reach her breast (Fig. 98). This statue was begun by Michelangelo in 1521, and no hands other than his worked on it. By 1534 it was left by its creator in its present incomplete state.

The marble was still in Michelangelo's workshop in the year 1549, as it had not yet been placed in the Medici Chapel.

Prior to 1944 there existed in the Kaiser Friedrich Museum (now the Staatliche Museum) in Berlin, a small, exquisitely sculptured terracotta model (Fig. 97) for the "Medici Madonna" marble statue in Florence.

Unfortunately, the clay model was smashed into splinters during the closing phase of World War II and only the very small, partly damaged head (Fig. 99) now remains intact.

The *Medici Madonna* marble statue in the Medici Chap
Florence, about 1521-1534. (*Opposit*

99 The Head of the *Medici Madonna*—terracotta model, surviving portion of the complete model, in the Staatliche Museum, Berlin.

100 The Head of the *Medici Madonna*, detail of the marble statue in the Medici Chapel, Florence.

101 A Bronze after a Model by Michelangelo of the *Medici Madonna*, in the Louvre, Paris, about 1790.

The face of the little model shows the same fixed gaze as that portrayed in the marble face (Fig. 100), with the exception that the face in clay appears to have been influenced to a slightly greater degree by antique sculptures of the female head and face.

There are large parts of the "Medici Madonna" marble statue which are unfinished, and this is particularly evident in the large block upon which the Virgin is seated. How Michelangelo meant the marble sculpture to look can be ascertained when a comparison is made of the completed block and base of the clay model, which has been executed in detail, with that of the incomplete marble in which the block and base are carved only in part. Other unfinished sections of the statue, such as the uncut portion of stone under the Virgin's left foot; the unfinished portions of her figure and robe, more especially her right arm; the Child's right foot; clearly demonstrate the fact that the far more detailed and complete sculpture in clay must have preceded the final one in stone.

There are two Michelangelo drawings (Figs. 102 and 104) over which art historians disagree as to whether or not they are actually preparatory drawings for the "Medici Madonna". Another area of disagreement concerns a 16th century drawing in the Louvre (Fig. 103) which may or may not have been made by Michelangelo as a preliminary sketch for the clay model. Herman Grimm believed that this drawing was by the hand of Michelangelo. Other authorities claim that it is not by the Master, but that it is a drawing by another artist after Michelangelo's preparatory model or the final figure in stone.

Figure 101 shows a sixteen-inch bronze replica of the "Medici Madonna", which was made in the 18th century or at the beginning of the 19th century. This rather inferior bronze casting originally comes from the Thiers Collection and is now in the Louvre. Because of certain variances, it cannot be a copy after the marble, and according to Goldscheider it may have been cast from an original Michelangelo model (*A Survey of Michelangelo's Models in Wax and Clay*, p. 55). There is little in the quality of the bronze which actually supports this supposition. Goldscheider in his book also reminds us that Henry Thode ("Michelangelo Kritische Untersuchungen über seine Werke", Vol. VI) mentions a tradition that Michelangelo presented this bronze statuette to the Archbishop of Florence, Giovanni Salviati, and adds that it remained in the Collection of the family until 1830.

The F. Schottmüller catalogue of 1933 states, p. 153, that the "Medici Madonna" clay model was acquired by the Kaiser Friedrich Museum in 1869 in Dresden and that it was formerly in the Praunsche Kabinett in Nuremberg.

The famous art historian, Herman Grimm, writing in 1879 (*Leben Michelangelos,* Vol. I, p. 488, and Vol. II, p. 552) says that the terracotta model for the "Medici Madonna" in Berlin was an authentic model by Michelangelo and lists it as having been formerly in the possession of Ernst Haehnel in Dresden. He further stated that the small clay figure had been covered with oil paint. The catalogue of the museum in Berlin emphasizes, however, that the model was of baked clay and unpainted and therefore it can be assumed that the paint was removed after Grimm had seen it.

102   (*Top left*) Two pen and ink sketches by Michelangelo for a *Madonna and Child*, in the Louvre, Paris, about 1524.

103   (*Above*) Sketch by Michelangelo of the *Medici Madonna*, in the Louvre, Paris, 16th Century.

104   *Madonna and Child*, pen and ink sketch by Michelangelo, in the Albertina, Vienna, about 1524.

The *Evening*

Height 7in. 178mm.
Length 12½ in. 318mm.

The whereabouts of the terracotta
model for the marble statue of
the "Evening" (Fig. 105), which
was never in the Haehnel Collection, but which was in the von
Praun Collection as stated in the
Murr Catalogue, has not been
known from the time that the
Praunsche Kabinett of Nuremberg was sold and dispersed in
1802. It can be assumed that by
the present time the model has
definitely been lost to posterity.

105   The *Evening*, marble statue in the Medici
Chapel, Florence, about 1524-1531.

Group II

Models for other well-known statues by the Master

The right arm of Christ in the *Pietà* in St. Peter's, Rome

Length 10½ in. 267 mm.

The wonderfully delicate terracotta model (Fig. 106) for the right arm of Christ in the "Pietà" in St. Peter's, Rome, which is now in the Victoria and Albert Museum, matches to a very close degree the right arm of the marble statue (Fig. 107). The arm of the clay model rests, however, on a narrow garment-like base, and this does not correspond with that in the original group, and the hand is bent a little more prominently at the wrist than in the statue.

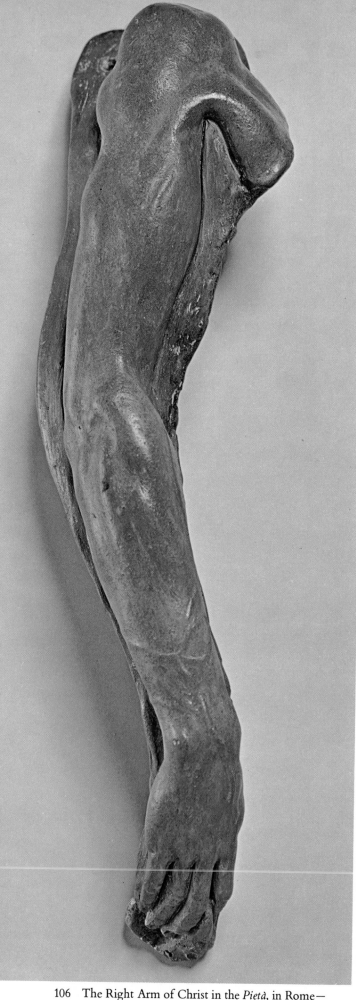

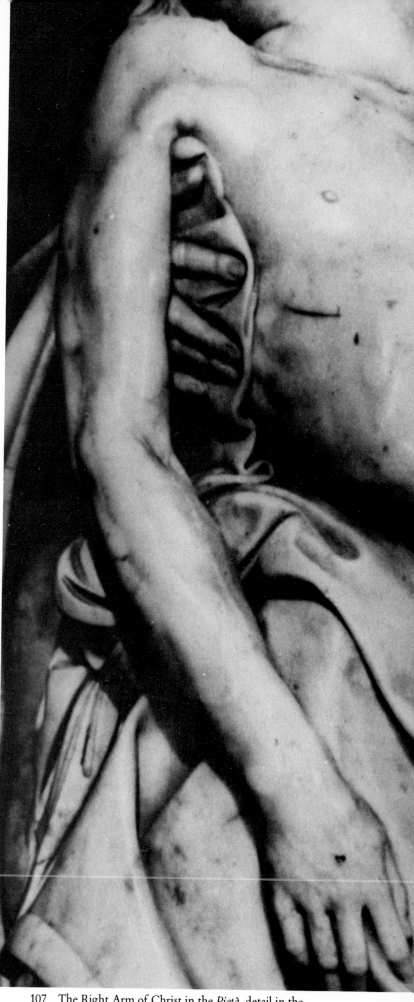

106 The Right Arm of Christ in the *Pietà*, in Rome—
terracotta model, in the Victoria and Albert Museum,
London, about 1498.

107 The Right Arm of Christ in the *Pietà*, detail in the
marble statue in St. Peter's, Rome, 1498-1499.

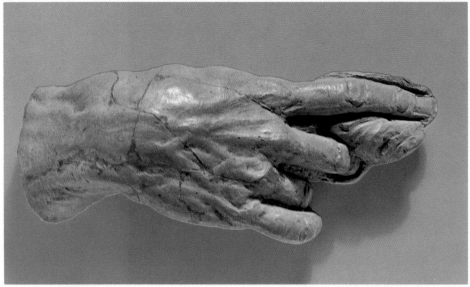

108
The Right Hand of *Moses*—
terracotta model, in the
Victoria and Albert Museum,
London, about 1513.

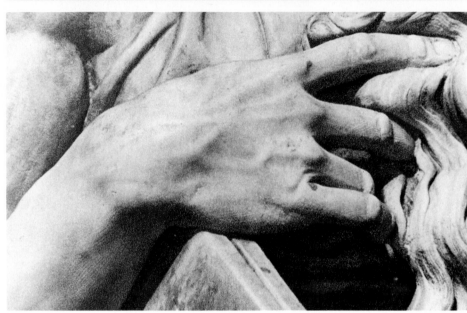

109
The Right Hand of *Moses*, detail of
the marble statue for the Tomb of
Pope Julius II, in San Pietro in
Vincoli, Rome, 1513-1516.

The right hand of *Moses*

Length 7½ in. 192mm.

The terracotta model of the right hand of "Moses" (Fig. 108), which is now in the Victoria and Albert Museum, matches in almost every detail the one in marble (Fig. 109), with the exception that the curl of the beard which is clasped by the forefinger and the middle finger is not clearly characterized in the model. Henry Thode was of the opinion that the model has the effect of a copy of the marble—it is too exact a replica. Thode further stated that it was rather doubtful that the model was created by Michelangelo. Other authorities are of a contrary opinion, however, because this particular model (as in the case of the model of the right hand of "Lorenzo de'Medici") shows clearly the use of a modelling rod on the fingernails, and because of the way it has been hollowed out at the back, it can be stated with conviction that it is an original clay model by the Great Master.

110 The Lower Body of *The Risen Christ*, in the Church of Santa Maria sopra Minerva—terracotta model, whereabouts unknown, about 1519.

111 The Lower Body of *The Risen Christ*, detail of the marble statue in the Church of Santa Maria sopra Minerva, Rome, 1519-1520.

The lower body of *The Risen Christ* in the Church of Santa Maria sopra Minerva

Height 12½ in. 318mm.

The present whereabouts of the model (Fig. 110) for the lower body (below the navel) of the marble sculpture of "Christ" (Fig. 111) in the Church of Santa Maria sopra Minerva, in Rome, is unknown.

The base and support behind the right leg was repaired by Haehnel. The position of the right foot of the model is slightly different to that of the statue, and the left leg of the model also seems to be placed further back than that in marble. This is one of the twelve models that Haehnel took with him to Florence on the occasion of the exhibition commemorating the four hundredth anniversary of Michelangelo's birth.

Because the clay model gives the impression of an imitation or copy of the marble, there is considerable doubt that it is the work of Michelangelo.

A study of a "Slave" for *The Julius Monument*   Height 7in. 178mm.

The present location of this model (Fig. 112), which is a study of a "Slave" for the "Julius Monument", is unknown.

The head of the model, the arms, the entire left leg and the right lower thigh are missing. The upper part of the body is turned to the right (Fig. 114). The arms are stretched upwards, and it appears that the

leg beneath the right knee is bent to a marked degree—in the manner of a forced position, which is consistent with that of a chained person. The position of the right leg, which must have been bent over the standing left leg, indicates that it is a study of a "Slave" intended for the "Julius Monument", similar to the ones that can be found

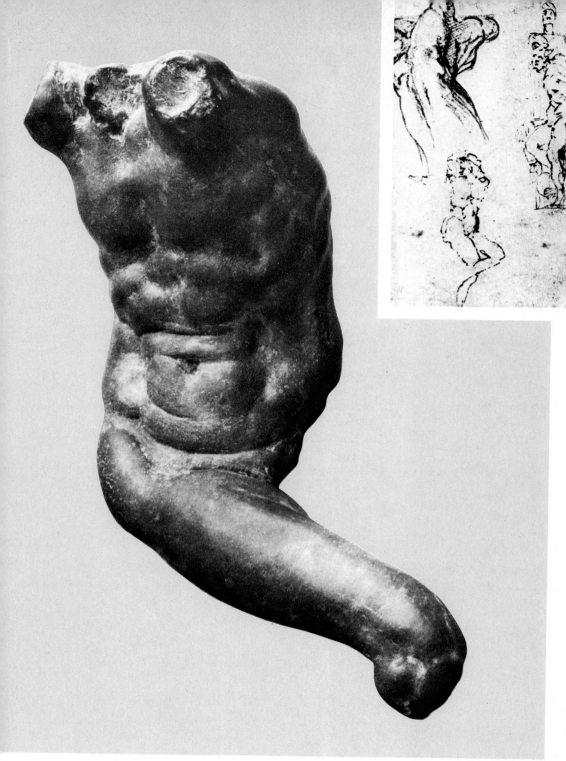

113 Studies by Michelangelo for *Captives* of *The Julius Monument* in the Ashmolean Museum, Oxford, about 1511-1513.

114
A Study of a *Slave* for *The Julius Monument* — terracotta model, whereabouts unknown.

in the famous drawing in The Ashmolean Museum Oxford (Fig. 113).

There are considerable differences between this model and the unfinished statues of the "Captives" from the Boboli Gardens in the Accademia, Florence. The model, however, may be only a variation of the motif as displayed in the Boboli statues.

Although the model is not directly related to a study of a torso (Fig. 4) by Michelangelo in the Casa Buonarroti, there is a remarkable similarity between them. A comparison between the clay model as shown in Figure 112 and the drawing of a torso as shown in Figure 29 should also be noted.

A straight standing right leg

(Reverse of the left leg of *The Risen Christ* in the church of Santa Maria sopra Minerva, Rome.)

Height 8-3/16in. 208mm.

The model (Fig. 115) of a straight standing right leg, without a foot but with part of the thigh, is executed with perfection and is now located in the Collection in Vancouver. The surface of this fine model (Fig. 116) shows the raised vein and muscle structure of the leg in the most realistic detail.

When the image of this beautifully sculptured clay model of a right leg is reversed (Figs. 116 and 117), one can recognize the left leg of the marble sculpture of "The Risen Christ" of the Church of Santa Maria sopra Minerva (Figs. 118 and 119).

The model was originally made solid, then cut in half while in the leather-hard stage, for hollowing-out purposes, and then rejoined prior to firing in a kiln. The model, which is completely hollow throughout, shows the scooping-out marks through the openings in its extremities. There is a small round hole for suspension purposes in the upper back portion of the model.

115 A Straight Standing Right Leg—terracotta model, in the Vancouver Collection, about 1519.

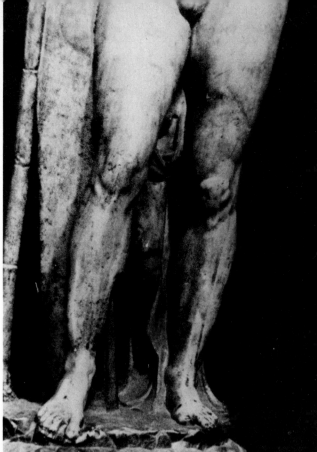

116 Mirror image of a Straight Standing Right Leg—
terracotta model, in the Vancouver Collection.

118 *The Risen Christ*, detail of the marble statue in the
Church of Santa Maria sopra Minerva, Rome, 1519-1520.

117 Mirror image of a Straight Standing Right Leg—
terracotta model, in the Vancouver Collection.

119 *The Risen Christ*, detail of the marble statue in the
Church of Santa Maria sopra Minerva, Rome.

120 A Torso of a Youth—terracotta model,
in the Vancouver Collection, about 1489.

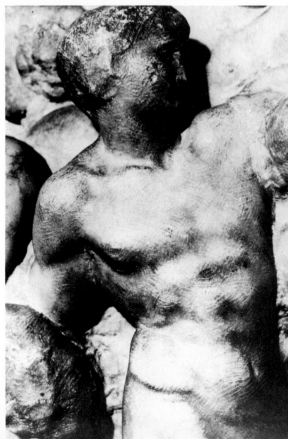

121
Battle of the Centaurs, detail of a figure in
marble relief, in the Casa Buonarroti, about 1492.

96

A torso of a youth

Height 4-5/8in. 115mm.

There is an exquisite small terracotta model (Fig. 120) of a torso in the Vancouver Collection. The arms, legs, and the head have not been sculptured, and the model has a reserved attitude, facing straight ahead, with a portion of the right arm directed upwards, whereas the left appears to be lowered.

Ludwig Goldscheider in his *Survey of Michelangelo's Models in Wax and Clay,* states that this is the only plastic study after the Greek style by Michelangelo that has come down to us. It belongs to his earlier period and it was used as a model for one of the figures in his marble relief "Battle of the Centaurs" (Fig. 122).

This particular study points to the fact that the greatest of all sculptors, at a very early age, took great pains to master in every detail, through careful studies, not only nature but also the "Antique" methods of form.

The model was made when the young Michelangelo entered Bertoldo's "School of Sculptors", which Lorenzo "The Magnificent" had established. Three years later the young sculptor executed the marble relief, the "Battle of the Centaurs" and used the model of the torso for one of the figures (Fig. 121) in it. The form of the torso (Figs. 120 and 128) can again be recognized several years later in some of the figures done for the "Battle of Cascina" as can be seen in the engraving (Fig. 123) after the lost cartoon, wherein the subject made very great demands upon the youthful artist's knowledge of the nude.

122 *Battle of the Centaurs*, marble relief, in the Casa Buonarroti, about 1492.

123 Engraving at Holkam Hall, England, after a copy of Michelangelo's lost cartoon for the *Battle of Cascina*, 1504-1505—British Museum, London.

124   A Torso of a Youth—terracotta model,
in the Vancouver Collection.

In this wonderfully executed
model (Fig. 124) one can see the
birth of Michelangelo's inspiration
and ability, which was so well
demonstrated twelve years later in
his "David" (Fig. 125).

There are numerous drawings
(Figs. 126, 127, 129, 130) by
Michelangelo which are similar in
many respects to the model (Figs.
124 and 128). This original clay
model by Michelangelo is hollow
throughout, having been cut in half
for scooping-out purposes and then
joined together prior to firing.
The model has a clay bridge
in its open base as a wall
support.

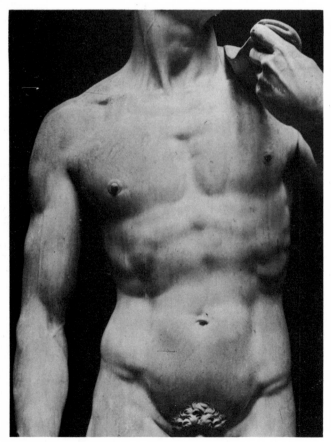

125   The *David*, detail of the marble statue in the
Accademia, Florence, 1501-1504.

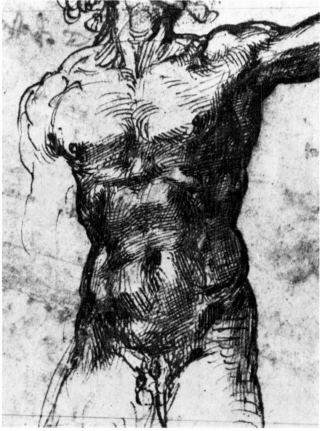

126   Nude Youth with Left Arm Extended, detail
of the drawing by Michelangelo in the British
Museum, about 1504.

127 The Back View of a Male Torso, detail of the drawing by Michelangelo in Oxford, about 1501.

129 Studies for the Nude, detail of the drawing by Michelangelo in Oxford, about 1502.

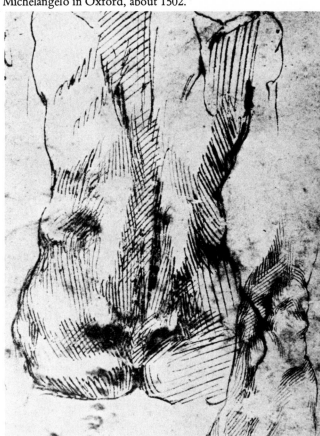

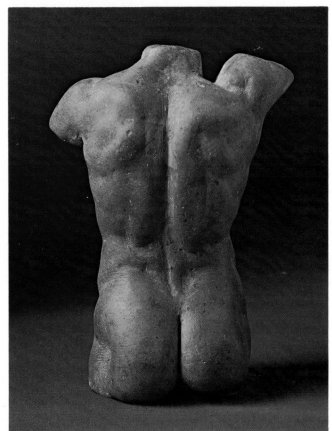

128 A Torso of a Youth (Back View)—terracotta model, in the Vancouver Collection.

130 A Male Torso, seen from the back (A Study by Michelangelo for *The Battle Cartoon*), in Vienna, about 1504.

A slender right leg

(The right leg of
The San Spirito Crucifix)

Length 6-13/16in. 173mm.

In the Vancouver Collection there is a terracotta model (Figs. 131 and 133) of a slender right leg, bent somewhat at the knee, which according to Henry Thode does not possess anything characteristic of Michelangelo's style. The toes have been damaged; nevertheless the downward bent pose of the foot indicates that the slim model is a generalized sketch of a right leg of a crucifix.

Until the identification ("Der Kruzifixus Michelangelos im Kloster Santo Spirito in Florenz", *Kunstchronik*, January, 1963) by M. Lisner, of the "San Spirito Crucifix" (thick coating of paint over wood) in the Casa Buonarroti, Florence (Fig. 132), as having been done by the hand of Michelangelo, it had not been possible to relate this unmuscular and slender model of a right leg to Michelangelo. Charles de Tolnay and U. Baldini (*The Complete Work of Michelangelo*, 1965) are in agreement with Lisner, that the "San Spirito Crucifix" is by Michelangelo. De Tolnay, in the same volume, p. 35, quotes Vasari: "If one wishes figures in wood to come out perfectly, he must first make a model in wax or clay". There is a remarkable similarity between the clay model and the legs of the wooden crucifix, both of which have not been developed to any great degree in their musculature, and both of which— as well as the total figure in wood of Christ on the cross—are not after the style of Michelangelo.

The terracotta colouring of this model is of a lighter, sandier nature than the great majority of the other models in the Haehnel-von Praun Collection, which are of reddish-brown colour. The interior of the upper thigh is hollow, with the scooping-out marks clearly discernible.

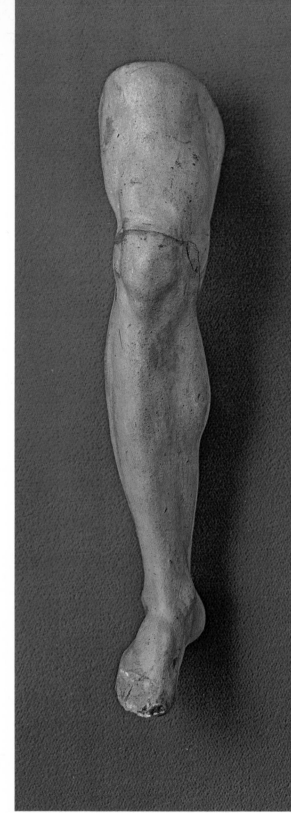

131   A Slender Right Leg—terracotta model, in the Vancouver Collection, about 1492.

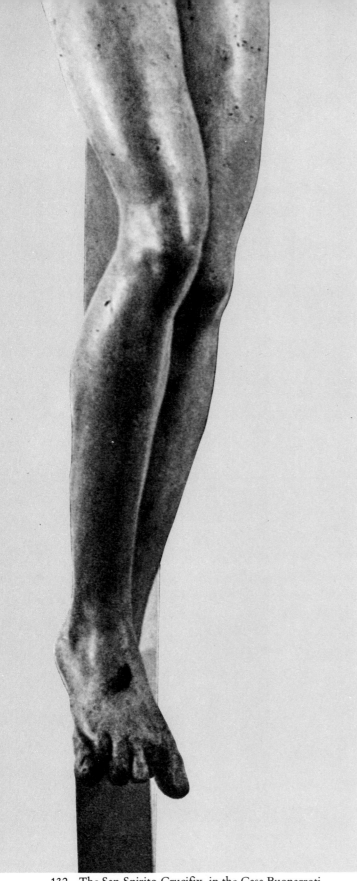

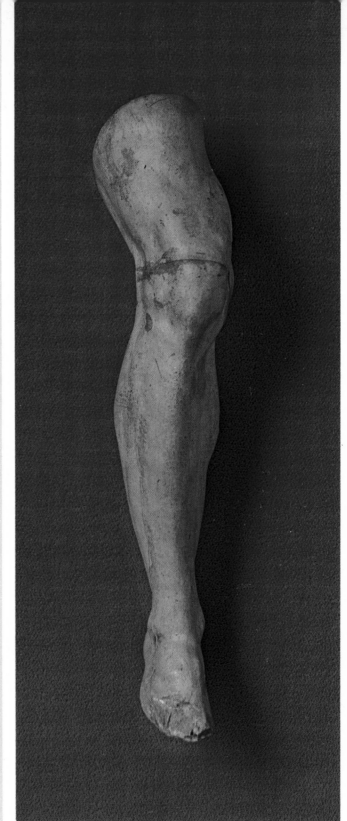

133   A Slender Right Leg—another view of the
terracotta model shown in Figure 131.

132   The San Spirito Crucifix, in the Casa Buonarroti,
Florence, 1492-1495.

A River God

(A first draft for the large model of a *River God* formerly in the Florence Accademia but now in the Casa Buonarroti, Florence)

Height 4in. 102mm.; Length 8in. 203mm.

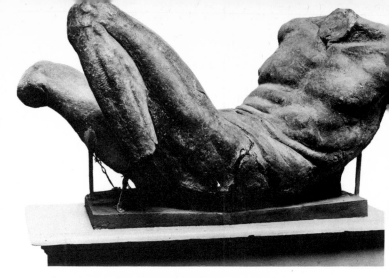

134 The Large Scale Clay Model of a *River God,* in the Casa Buonarroti, Florence, about 1525.

It is known that for each large-scale clay or gesso (plaster of Paris) model (Fig. 134—seventy inches long) that Michelangelo made, he also made at least two small models. The Master normally made at first a small rough sketch, such as the wax model (Fig. 135—five inches long) of a "River God", now in the British Museum, and then sculptured a well-finished work in clay such as the terracotta model of a "River God" (Fig. 136—eight inches long), at one time in the Haehnel-von Praun Collection, but which has now disappeared.

It is only within the last sixty-five years that the large full-sized clay model of a "River God", now in the Casa Buonarroti, has been judged by art historians as being by the hand of Michelangelo, and not by Bartolommeo Ammanati (1511-1592) as was its previous attribution. De Tolnay says of the great "River God": "Stylistically, in the richness of the modelling of the torso and

legs, the 'River God' is a far cry from the simple surfaces of Ammanati's sculptures". Gottschewski was the first to recognize the large "River God" (Figs. 134 and 137) as an original full-scale terrasecca model by Michelangelo. It should be noted that the Haehnel Collection included a small terracotta model (Fig. 138) of the "River God" and that Adolf Gottschewski, writing in 1905 an article ("Ein Original-Tonmodell Michelangelos"), was very impressed by the Haehnel Collection.

Thode at first thought that the small model was a copy of the larger full-scale model in the Florence Accademia and wrote to this effect. After considerable further study, however, he came to the definite conclusion that the small model was a first draft of the great model in Florence, which is the only extant full-sized model by Michelangelo.

The art historian, Hans Mackowsky,

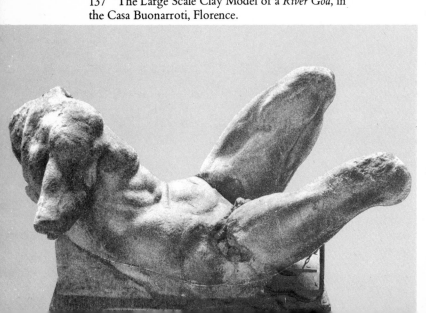

137 The Large Scale Clay Model of a *River God*, in the Casa Buonarroti, Florence.

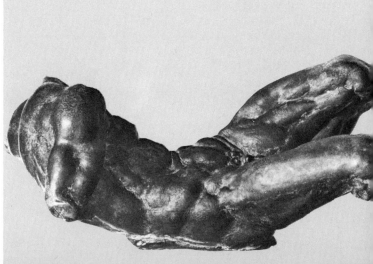

138 A First Draft for the Large Model of a *River God* in the Casa Buonarroti—terracotta model, whereabouts unknown.

135 The Wax Sketch of a *River God*, in The British Museum, London, about 1525.

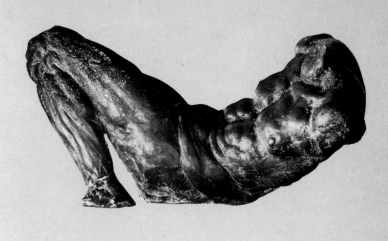

136 A First Draft for the Large Model of a *River God* in the Casa Buonarroti—terracotta model, whereabouts unknown, about 1525.

wrote in 1919 (*Michelagniolo*) that the large model (clay, to which shearing has been added) of the "River God" in Florence, which had been considerably damaged, must have been made in Michelangelo's workshop from a small model by the Master. It can be assumed that the more complete small terracotta model of a "River God" in the Haehnel-von Praun Collection was the small model that Mackowsky was contemplating. It is known from Michelangelo's own letters and records that between 1524 and March of 1526, Michelangelo had finished eight full-scale models for the Medici Chapel, namely, for the two "Medici", the four "Phases of the Day", and for two "River Gods". The small models for the statues, therefore, must have been finished before this period. Cellini, the Florentine sculptor and goldsmith, stated that he had seen models by Michelangelo in the sacristy of San Lorenzo.

Gottschewski mentions in his article on

Michelangelo's large-scale "River God", quoting from an article by Müntz, that on June 13, 1559, several works of art were in the writing room of Duke Cosimo, of which the "River God" was the original by the hand of Michelangelo himself.

The small model from the Haehnel-von Praun Collection is considerably more complete than the full-sized model, and this is most noticeable when a comparison is made of both left legs below the knee. The small torso is vastly superior in workmanship with respect to the detailed sculpturing of the anatomy. The same can be said when a comparison is made between this model and a similar one in wax (Fig. 4) in the Casa Buonarroti. The remarkable similarity between the small clay model in the von Praun Collection and the "Belvedere Torso" (Fig. 139) which Michelangelo knew well, demonstrates in a direct way the manner in which Michelangelo was influenced by the "Antique".

Under nos. 33, 34 and 35 of the index for terracottas of the Murr Catalogue, the models are identified as three "River Gods". Only one of these "River Gods", illustrated in Figures 136 and 138, was in the Haehnel Collection and it is indeed a pity that along with the other two, formerly in the von Praun Collection, it has also disappeared.

139 The Belvedere Torso, Roman copy in marble, Vatican Museum, Rome, about 150 B.C.

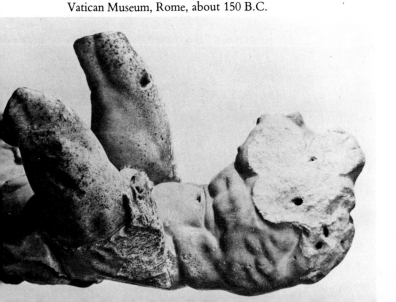

103

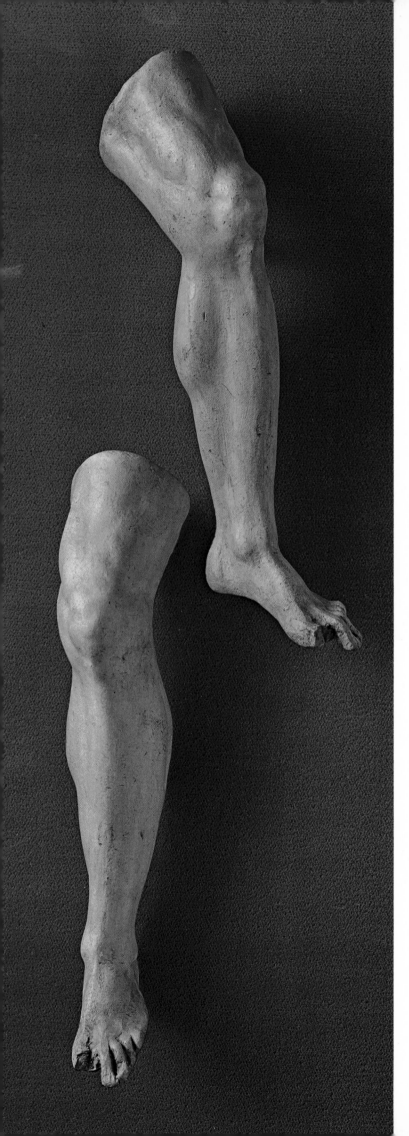

A slender left leg

(The left leg of Christ in the *Pietà,* Rome)

Length 6-39/64in. 168mm.

In this terracotta model of a slender left leg
(Fig. 140) in the Canadian Collection, can be
discerned a very close relationship to the left leg
of the marble statue of Christ in the "Pietà" in
Rome (Fig. 141). The relationship is particularly
evident with respect to the slender instep and
somewhat elongated arch of the foot—a rare
sculpturing method of Michelangelo's which
appears most noticeably in this model and in the
finished sculpture in stone.

   The slender proportions of the clay model
are very similar to those of the left leg of Christ
in marble. Comparison shows, however, that
the model is a little less bent at the knee and
that the big toe has been broken off. It could
also have been envisaged by Michelangelo as a
model for the left leg of a Crucifix.

   This clay model is of a light sandy colour,
with the interior of the upper thigh having
been hollowed out and the resultant interior
scooping-out marks quite distinguishable.

140   A Slender Left Leg—terracotta model in the
Vancouver Collection, about 1498.

141   The Left Leg of Christ, detail of the marble
Pietà in St. Peter's, Rome, 1498-1499.

An erect standing left leg

(A first draft of the left leg of *The Risen Christ*)

Height 7-5/16in. 186mm.

According to Henry Thode, the erect standing clay model of a left leg (Fig. 142), now in the Canadian Collection, is very closely related to the model for "Christ" in the Church of Santa Maria sopra Minerva (Fig. 110) in the Haehnel-von Praun Collection, both as to its form and in its execution.

The light-toned terracotta model has a small round hole in its upper back portion for suspension purposes. It was cut in half while in a leather-hard state to facilitate the scooping-out of its hollow interior. Scooping-out marks are clearly visible through an opening in the upper thigh of the model, and it is completely hollow except at the extreme base of the leg, which is solid. It is very probable that this model was cast from an original wax model.

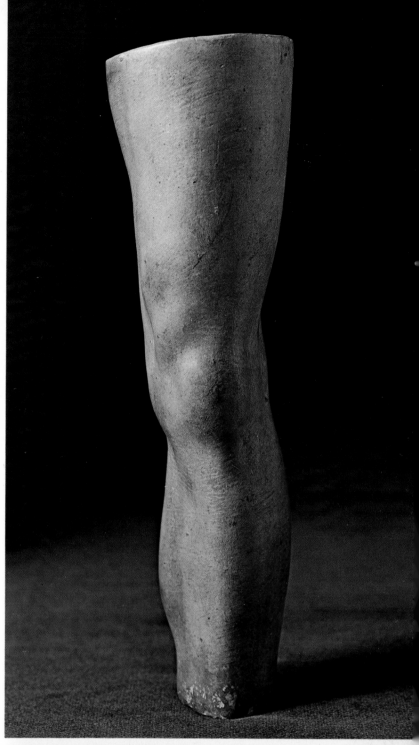

142
An Erect Standing Left Leg—terracotta model, in the Vancouver Collection, about 1513.

A left foot with part of the leg

Height 3-1/32in. 78mm.

According to Thode, the terracotta model (Fig. 143) of a foot with part of the leg, now in the Canadian Collection, very possibly belongs to the model of an erect standing leg (Fig. 142) which was also formerly in the Haehnel Collection. His statement that the breakage does not fit exactly, however, is open to argument. The model is solid throughout.

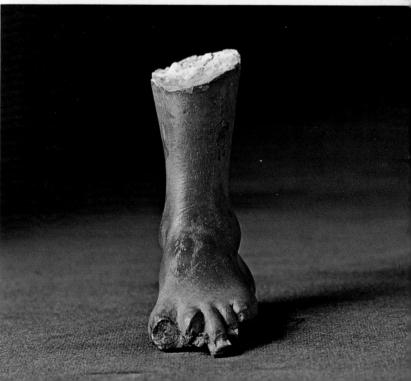

143
A Left Foot with Part of the Leg—terracotta model, in the Vancouver Collection, about 1513.

144 Four Michelangelo Models, detail of the painting *Sight* (25½ins. by 43ins.) by Jan Brueghel the *Elder*, in the Prado, Madrid, about 1617.

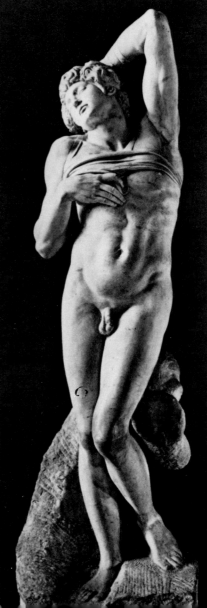

145
The Heroic Captive, marble statue in the Louvre, Paris, 1514-1516.

146
The Dying Captive, marble statue, in the Louvre, Paris, 1514-1516.

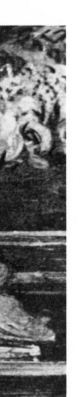

Two "Slaves" for the *Julius Monument*

Height approx. 16in. 407mm.

Figure 144 is a small section of a painting showing four models by Michelangelo. The painting called "Sight", is by Jan Brueghel the "Elder" (1568-1625) and it is one of a series of five painted around the year 1617 and which are now in the Prado Museum in Madrid. The two outer figures on the shelf represent the models for the "Night" and for the "Dawn" in the Medici Chapel. The two inner figures represent the models for the "Heroic Captive" on the left, and the "Dying Captive" on the right, and both of these models were for marble sculptures which were originally intended for the "Pope Julius Monument" and which are now located in the Louvre.

In comparing the relative sizes of other objects in the painting, it can be estimated that the two models for the Medici Tomb figures are approximately 7 inches high and 12 inches long, and therefore correspond to the size of the two models from the von Praun Collection. It can also be estimated that each of the two "Captive" models shown in the painting were approximately 16 inches high.

There were two terracotta models in the von Praun Collection which, it can be assumed, were for the two marble figures, the "Heroic Captive" (Fig. 145) and the "Dying Captive" (Fig. 146). Both models are classified in Murr's Catalogue of 1797 as Captives ("Prigioni") by the hand of Michelangelo—under nos. 41 and 42.

Neither model was in the Haehnel Collection and it is presumed that they were both lost early in the nineteenth century.

St. Bartholomew

Height 24in. 610mm.

A model of a two-foot high anatomical clay study was at one time in the von Praun Collection, and it was supposedly for the marble statue of St. Bartholemew in Milan Cathedral, according to the attribution following no. 43 in p. 241 of the 1797 Murr Catalogue of the von Praun Collection, where it is stated to be by Michelangelo.

The model was never in the Haehnel Collection and it can be presumed that it disappeared early in the nineteenth century.

Group III

Studies by Michelangelo after the "Antique", or of a character according to the "Antique"

A left bent arm with a bordering part of the breast and back

Height 4½in. 115mm.

The terracotta model (Fig. 147) of a left bent arm with a bordering part of the breast and back is now missing. It is related in its form to the clay model for a left arm, shoulder and part of the back (Fig. 31) now in Vancouver and also from the von Praun Collection.

In the opinion of Henry Thode, a hand was never completed for the model and therefore the action cannot be clearly defined. He further states that it can at best be characterized as the action of a rower. A comparison of the model, however, with the marble figure of "The Risen Christ" (Fig. 148) shows that the uncompleted hand of the arm of the model was very possibly meant to hold an upright cross. Except for the variance in the bend of the arm, there exists a remarkable similarity between the marble statue and the clay model, with the likelihood that the latter was made by Michelangelo specifically as a study for the statue.

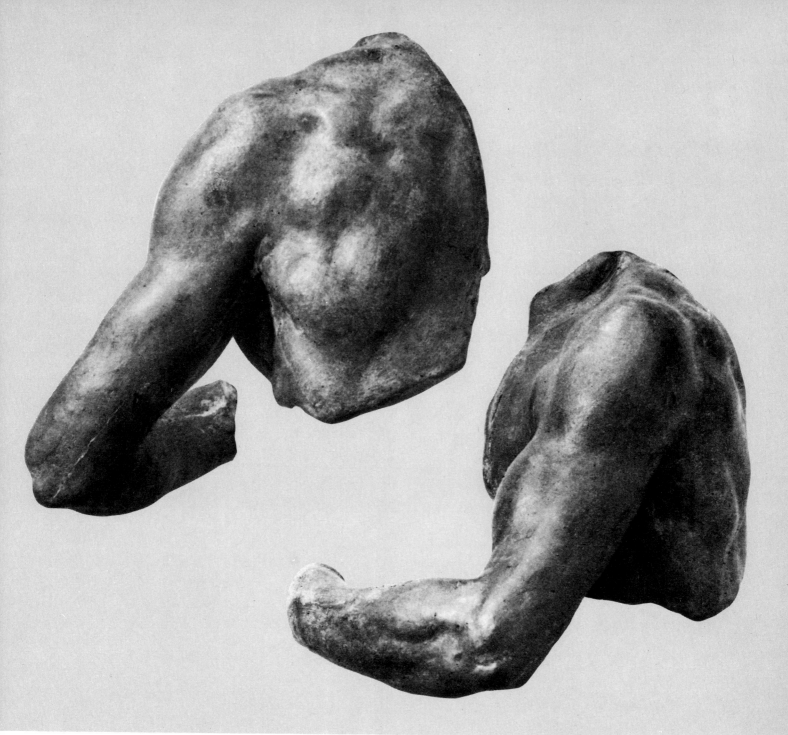

147 A Left Bent Arm with a Bordering Part of the Breast and Back—two views of the terracotta model, whereabouts unknown.

148 *The Risen Christ*—two views of the marble statue in the Church of Santa Maria sopra Minerva, Rome, about 1519-1520.

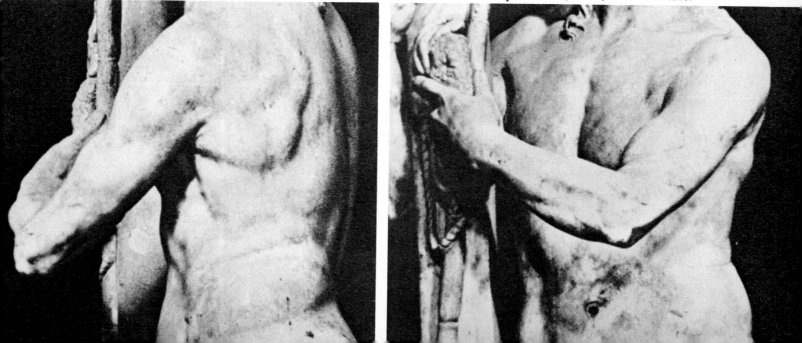

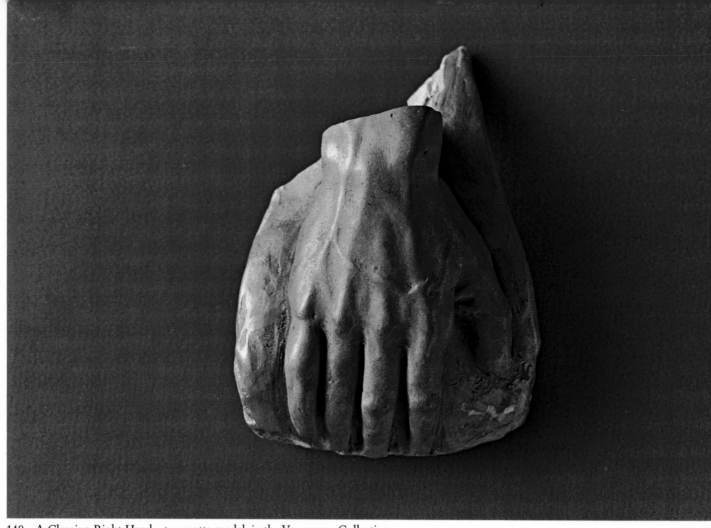

149 A Clasping Right Hand—terracotta model, in the Vancouver Collection.

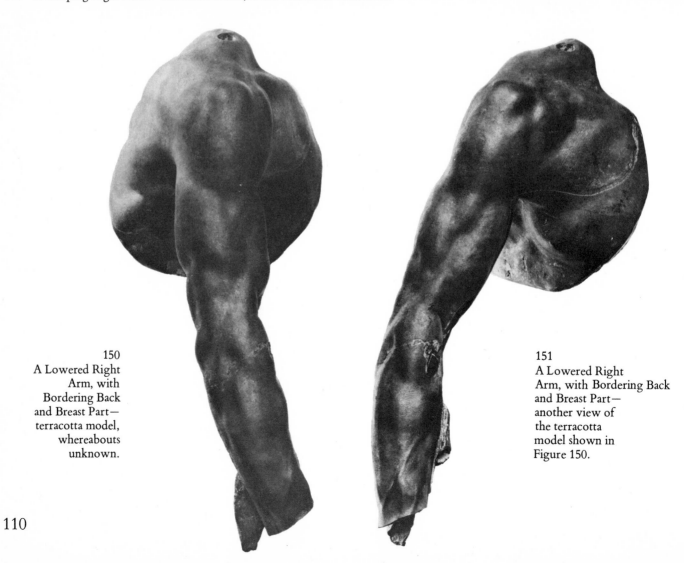

150
A Lowered Right
Arm, with
Bordering Back
and Breast Part—
terracotta model,
whereabouts
unknown.

151
A Lowered Right
Arm, with Bordering Back
and Breast Part—
another view of
the terracotta
model shown in
Figure 150.

A lowered right arm and clasping hand, with the bordering back and breast part

Total length 20in. 508mm.; height of hand 4-3/16in. 107mm.

In the Vancouver Collection there is a terracotta model (Fig. 149) of a clasping right hand. This hand is part of a larger model (Figs. 150 and 151) of a lowered right arm with the bordering back and breast part, which has now disappeared. The photograph of the completed model in Thode's article on the Haehnel Collection shows the hand attached to the arm, and no apparent break between them. Meier-Graefe, however, illustrates the two parts separately and it can therefore be assumed that the breakage must have taken place between 1913 and 1924. The completed model has a hole in the top part of it for suspension purposes.

Thode mistakenly regarded the complete model as a copy by Michelangelo after the right arm and hand of "Menelaos" in the Roman copy of the Greek marble grouping of "Menelaos Holding the Dead Body of Patroklos" in the Loggia della Signoria, Florence. The marble group came to Florence in 1570, soon after it was excavated in Rome, and therefore six years after the death of Michelangelo.

The fingernails of the terracotta hand have been incompletely sculptured. Of particular interest, however, is the beautifully executed surface vein structure of the clay hand, and the fact that a somewhat similar surface vein design appears in the right hand of "Moses" in marble (Fig. 109).

Although the arm and shoulder are no longer available for examination purposes, it would appear after study of the hand that the complete model was originally made solid throughout, with the breast part having been hollowed out at its back, as is the case of the model for the left arm, shoulder and part of the back of "Evening" in the Vancouver Collection (Fig. 31). There is also a possibility that the complete model may have been cast by Michelangelo from an original wax model by him, as the patina of the model of the hand appears to be somewhat waxy, and a seam appears in the photographic reproduction of the arm and breast. There is a remarkable similarity between the clay model of the arm and breast and that shown in a pen and black crayon drawing by Michelangelo, reproduced in Figure 152.

152 Study by Michelangelo for the *Sistine Chapel Fresco*, detail of a lowered right arm with bordering breast part, in the Institute of Arts, Detroit, about 1508.

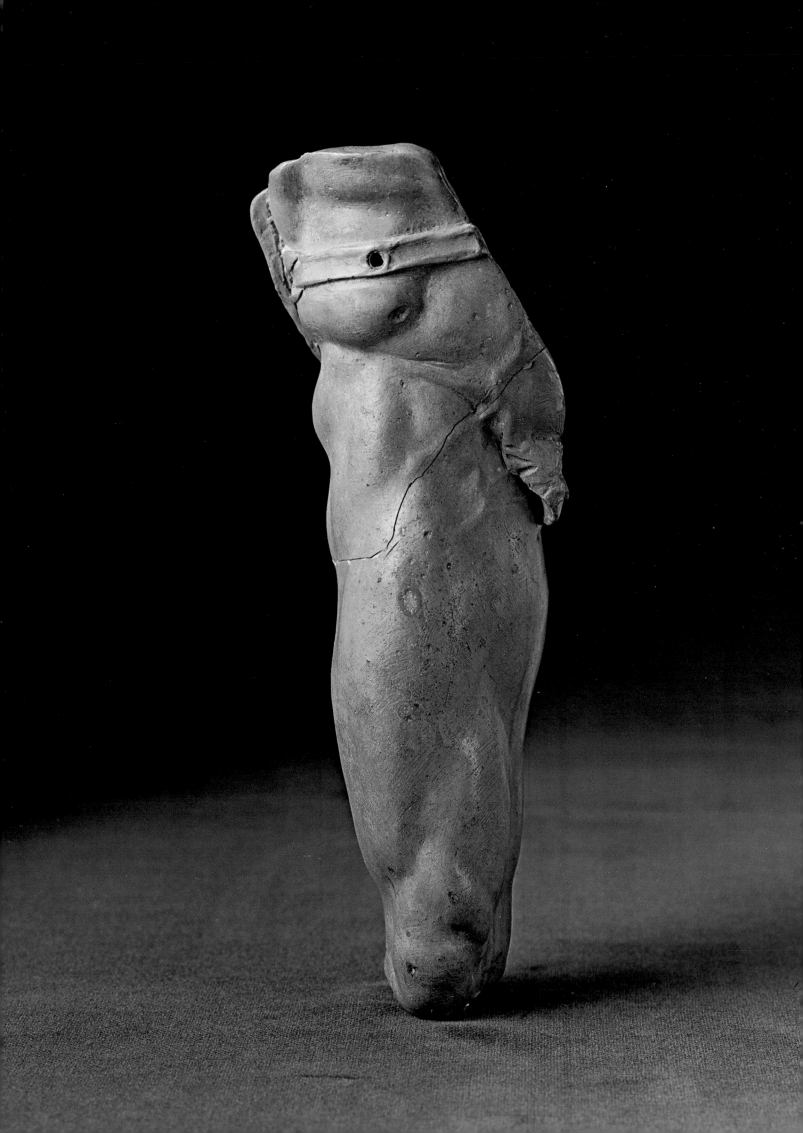

A right thigh, knee and part of a male body

Height 9¼in. 235mm.

The Vancouver Collection includes a very finely executed model (Fig. 153) of a right thigh, knee, and part of a male body. There is a piece of material with the appearance of leather behind the back, which is tightened to the body with the help of a thong. According to Thode, this model has the same perfection and flow of forms as the model (Fig. 88) for the left thigh of a reclining figure and it might have been made at the same time.

The sculptured form of the terracotta shows that the related torso would be leaning slightly forward from the waist, with its leg somewhat bent below the knee, or alternatively the torso would be in an erect position with its thigh placed a little to the fore.

This beautifully made model, with its detailed veins standing out on its surface, is a study after the "Antique" and very possibly for a "Slave", which was contemplated but never completed in marble by Michelangelo. Similar parts of a male body (without the leather thong around the waist) can be seen in drawings by Michelangelo and in his "Last Judgment" fresco. It is of interest to note that Michelangelo's "Heroic Captive" in the Louvre also has a thin leather thong sculptured closely to the body at its waist, but in a lower position than that in the model.

A crack across the middle of the model shows that at one time it was broken into two parts. The break must have occurred after 1924, as it does not appear in Meier-Graefe's photo-engraving of the model.

This original clay model was partly cut, for scooping-out purposes, while in its leather-hard stage. The scooping-out marks can be clearly discerned on the interior walls of the model.

53 A Right Thigh, Knee and Part of a Male Body— terracotta model, in the Vancouver Collection. (*Opposite*).

154   A Torso of a Male—terracotta model, in the Vancouver Collection, about 1492.

A torso of a male

Height 8-1/16in. 204mm.

One of the very best examples of the influence of the "Antique" on Michelangelo is demonstrated in the model (Fig. 154) of a torso of a male, now in the Canadian Collection. The head and the lower thighs were never made for this torso. The right arm ends just above the elbow, and there is but a short piece of the upper left arm attached to the torso. The left arm is extended to the side, a little lowered from the horizontal. The right arm is extended downwards, in a manner which indicates that it might be supported, as the arm's right shoulder is raised a little. The thighs are in a partially closed position with the right thigh a little ahead of the left. Henry Thode in his August 1913 *Monatshefte für Kunstwissenschaft* article stated:

> "The magnificent figure is of antique impression, the impression of Praxiteles, only richer and fuller in its forms, in a similar way, as Michelangelo built them on his Bacchus."

Although Michelangelo may not have seen Roman copies of statuary by Praxiteles, this model with the well known "Praxiteles Curve" has a remarkable resemblance to the style and bearing of Praxiteles' "Resting Satyr", to his "Young Satyr Pouring Wine", and to the reverse position of his "Hermes". These statues by Praxiteles were, however, unearthed long after the death of Michelangelo.

A very fine similarity exists between the clay model and an ink drawing (Fig. 155) by Michelangelo in "Antique Style", as well as with the drawing (Fig. 156) of Mercury-Apollo in the Paris Louvre.

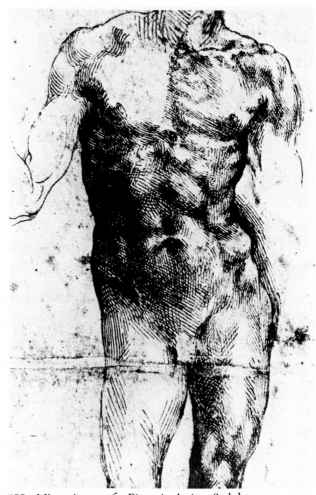

155 Mirror image of a *Figure in Antique Style* by Michelangelo, in the Louvre, Paris, between 1496 and 1500.

There is a pen drawing (Fig. 157) in the Louvre by Rubens, which is a copy of Michelangelo's lost "Hercules". The statue of "Hercules" by Michelangelo passed from the Palazzo Strozzi to the King of France. In the time of Henry IV it was at Fontainebleau, but nothing has been heard of it since 1713. Michelangelo was seventeen when he made this first larger-than-life size figure in marble, which directly anticipated the marble "David".

Charles de Tolnay in his *The Art and Thought of Michelangelo* compares the marble statue of "Bacchus" (Fig. 158) by Michelangelo after the "Antique", with the drawing by Rubens of the lost marble "Hercules" by the same sculptor. Although the comparison is valid, the resemblance is far greater between the "Hercules" drawing and the model of the male torso in the Canadian Collection. The stances are the same (left hips protruding sideways, with right hips slightly forward) as are their attitudes—upper part of both bodies turned slightly to the left, with their right legs slightly forward. The left dipping line of the shoulders is also similar in both cases, as is the position of both necks. The breasts in the drawing are a little more full, as in the terracotta model, than in the "Bacchus".

Although there is a fine similarity between the clay model and the marble statue of "Bacchus", especially as they are both softly, almost femininely, sculptured and have somewhat the same attitudes, the comparisons between the model and the Rubens drawing of the lost "Hercules" by Michelangelo are truly remarkable. The body moulding and the "Praxiteles Curve" in both the Rubens drawing and the model are almost replicas. The importance of

The *Bacchus*, marble statue in the Museo Nazionale
del Bargello, Florence, 1496-1497.

the terracotta clay model in Vancouver
cannot be underestimated, as it forms a
direct link, through the "Hercules" drawing by Rubens, to the lost statue of "Hercules" by Michelangelo.

According to Charles de Tolnay (*The
Complete Work of Michelangelo*, p. 15)
there is a wax statuette (Fig. 159) in the
Casa Buonarroti, Florence, which formerly was believed to be a study for the marble "David", but which he says is actually
a model for the lost "Hercules". As previously pointed out, this wax model,
judging from photographs as well as from
the personal examination of it made by
Sir Eric Maclagan and other experts of his
time (*Burlington Magazine*, Vol. XLIV,
1924, pp. 4 to 16), was cast from a mould;
seams are indicated along its length and
there is an iron spike protruding from its
head. In that the overall effect of Rubens'
pen drawing of Michelangelo's lost "Hercules" (Fig. 157) is that of a statue of
Antiquity, the comparison between the
"Hercules" drawing and the wax statuette
in the Casa Buonarroti is not nearly as
significant as that between the "Hercules"
drawing and the terracotta torso in the
Vancouver Collection (Fig. 154).

While in the leather-hard stage of drying, this original clay model by the Great
Master which is now in Vancouver, was
cut in half along the length of the torso
for scooping-out purposes, and then joined together prior to firing in a kiln. The
model has a small round hole at the nape
of the neck for suspension purposes and,
since 1924, when a photo-engraving was
made by Meier-Graefe, it has been repaired at its base and buttocks with plaster, and has been placed on a stand.

A Wax Statuette, in the Casa Buonarroti, Florence, about 1504.

A torso of a standing youth

Height 10½in. 267mm.

The terracotta model (Fig. 160) of a torso of a standing youth is now missing. The head, arms and feet were never intended to be a part of the model. The left leg is placed across the right at the knees, the left arm appears to be raised and the right arm can perhaps be presumed to move to the side and across the breast of the model. The right side of the small of the back is damaged, and according to Henry Thode, broken single pieces were later attached with glue. As with the marble "Bacchus" (Fig. 158) and the model of a torso of a male (Fig. 154) in the Vancouver Collection, the form of the clay torso is full, soft, and somewhat feminine.

Thode was of the opinion that the model was done in Michelangelo's early period as it is very similar to the youths leaning against the parapet in the background of his "Madonna Doni" painting. The position of the lower part of the body, and the thighs and legs indicate that it might have been a first study for the "Dying Captive" (Fig. 161) in the Louvre. This possibility was also considered by Thode. In his 1913 article on the Haehnel Collection, however, he added:

"Yet the model may still belong to an earlier period. The fine sense of forms corresponds with the Antique, the motif of movement is according to Michelangelo."

Henry Thode reported that a small piece of paper had been found in the interior of this terracotta model, and wrote in his 1913 article of the event:

"It may further be noted that after Paul von Praun's death no further purchases have been made for his art cabinet, which means that the models must have been acquired all by himself.

"Fortunately we can gain a more definite answer as to their origin from a small discovery

160   A Torso of a Standing Youth—terracotta model, whereabouts unknown.

recently made. On a transport from Berlin to Dresden that has recently been carried out, one of the terracottas, the statue of a male youth, opened itself right through the middle, and in its hollow interior a small slip of paper let in with great care was found which had its origin in the 16th century without a doubt. On the bottom of this paper is an inscription, although worn but still recognizable and written in lapis, where I am able to read

) o peʃʒι ι ι

from: 10 (?) pezzi—then still two more signs follow, one of which resembles an '1', whereas the second one is so blurred that a definite presumption cannot be made anymore. Perhaps these two signs were an indication of the price.

"As hazardous as it would be to draw a casting information on these few letters, yet I am compelled to stress the fact that the steep line of the writing would without hesitation be declared genuine, if it were found on any drawing by the Master. Whoever would not be shy to be called daring may eventually go so far as to declare: there is one proof for the genuineness of the models. However, I should not like to be a party to such daring."

The complete irregular breakage across the middle of the model that Thode speaks of is easily discernible. A side view of the model (Fig. 162) clearly shows the line of cut (down the side and length of the model) that was employed in this model, and in many others made by Michelangelo, so that he could hollow out the clay from its interior prior to turning it into terracotta through the firing process.

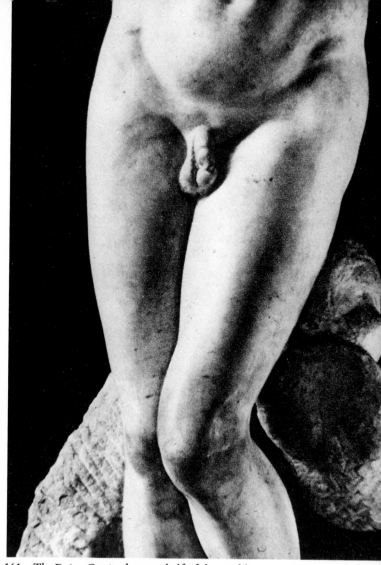

161 *The Dying Captive,* bottom half of the marble statue in the Louvre, Paris, 1514-1516.

162
A Torso of a Standing Youth—terracotta model, whereabouts unknown.

A torso of a youth

Height 7in. 178mm.

The model (Fig. 163) of a torso of a youth, which has a very similar style and form to that shown in Figure 154 is now missing and neither does it appear in a photographic reproduction attached to Henry Thode's article in 1913 on the Haehnel Collection. Thode does state, however, with reference to the model:

> "Torso of a youth. The head and the arms are missing. The left leg is only preserved up to a little above the knee; from the right leg only half the thigh is preserved. The figure reminds us of the Sauroktonos by Praxiteles."

A black crayon and pen sketch (Fig. 164) in the British Museum, lightly drawn by Michelangelo about 1504, is almost identical to the clay model and it can be assumed that they were both executed by Michelangelo around the same time.

163   A Torso of a Youth—terracotta model, whereabouts unknown.

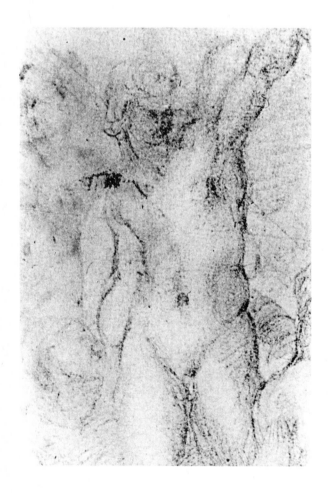

164
Study by Michelangelo for *The Battle Cartoon*, detail, in the British Museum, London, about 1504.

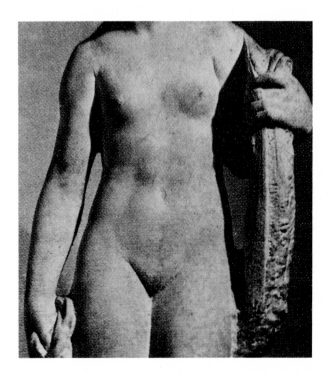

165   A Torso of a Young Woman—terracotta
model, whereabouts unknown.

A torso of a young woman

Height 5in. 127mm.

This model (Fig. 165) of a young woman is
now missing. It must have been lost since
Thode wrote about it in 1913, and prior to
1924 when Meier-Graefe failed to record its
photograph. No record appears of the
model at the Christie's sale in 1938.

The torso has been modelled without
the head, arms or both legs except the upper
thigh parts. The upper part of the body is
somewhat lowered towards its right side,
and the left arm appears to be extended
upwards.

According to Henry Thode, this wonderfully Psyche-like torso also owes its creation
to the study of the "Antique". He is reminded of early Venus studies by the
Master, in particular that of a sketch in the
British Museum.

The marble statue of Venus with two
cupids (Fig. 166) in the Casa Buonarroti,
and ascribed in part (the two cupids) to
Michelangelo in its 1970 catalogue, shows a
remarkable similarity to the terracotta
model, and illustrates the influence of the
"Antique" on Michelangelo.

166
A portion of the marble *Venus*
(see *Commentari,* Charles de Tolnay, 1966,
pp. 324 and foll.) Casa Buonarroti, Florence,
about 1496.

A bas-relief by Michelangelo

Height 10in. 259mm.
Width 5in. 128mm.

167
Haman, detail of a corner spandrel (Esther and Haman, 1511), Sistine Chapel Ceiling, Rome.

Under no. 76 of the Index for terracottas, in the Murr Catalogue of the von Praun Collection, there is mention of a terracotta rectangular bas-relief by Michelangelo which is a study of the fresco painting of "Haman" (Fig. 167) in a corner spandrel of the ceiling of the Sistine Chapel.

Under no. 98 of the Index for pictures of the same Catalogue, follows the description of a painting on canvas by Michelangelo, 1 ft 9 in. high by 10 in. wide, which is also a study of "Haman":

> "Haman dans un angle de la Chapelle Sixtine du Vatican. Voyez *Vasari* T. VI. p. 212. Flor. 1772, 4 . . . . On trouve le même sujet en terre cuite parmi les Études de ce grand Maître dans ce Cabinet. Voyez les Modèles N. 76, et parmi les *Estampes,* Portefeuille C. n. 233."

Nothing has been heard of this terracotta bas-relief since, as noted above, it was reported to be in the von Praun Collection. As previously stated in this volume there exists a similarity between the left thigh and knee of "Haman" in the Sistine Chapel ceiling painting and that of the terracotta model shown in Figure 92, as well as to the drawing shown in Figure 95.

The Murr Catalogue lists under no. 74 of the Index for terracotta a bas-relief, 1ft 7in. high by 10in. wide, of the "Libyan Sibyl" (or the "Cumaean Sibyl") holding a book in her hands. Under no. 78 of the same Index a bas-relief is identified as: "A man lying down—a figure for the Medici Tombs". Although these two reliefs are not directly identified in the catalogue as being by the hand of Michelangelo, and although they have disappeared since the breaking-up of the Praunsche Kabinett it can be assumed that they were actually modelled by Michelangelo, primarily because of their direct connection to his finished works and secondly because they are listed with the other bas-reliefs in terracotta under the heading: "Divers bas-reliefs de Michel-Ange, et d'autres".

168   A Plaquette after a design in wax by Michelangelo—terracotta relief, in the museum attached to the University of California, about 1560.

A plaquette after a design in wax by Michelangelo

Height 4½in. 115mm.; Width 5in. 128mm.

In the museum attached to the University of California there is a terracotta plaque (Fig. 168) of "Hercules and Atlas", which according to Ludwig Goldscheider comes from the Leoni bottega, and was very likely cast by Leoni (a favourite student of Michelangelo's) from a wax sketch made by Michelangelo. There were two other wax designs which Leoni received about the same time (1560) from Michelangelo in order to cast two bronze medals from them.

The plaquette, which was sold at the same Christie's auction in which the Michelangelo models were sold, and which was also in the von Praun Collection, was illustrated in the frontispiece of the excellent catalogue of the Sigmund Morgenroth Collection of "Medals and Plaquettes" exhibited at The Art Institute of Chicago in 1944. In the catalogue the plaquette was attributed on a questionable basis to Prospero Sogari (1516-1584) by the noted authority Ulrich Middledorf.

Thode, in his 1913 article on the models by Michelangelo in the Haehnel Collection, did not consider the plaquette to have come from the hand of Michelangelo. He stated that the muscles were too strong and too unpleasant—exaggerated in the manner of the sculptor Bandinelli (1488-1560).

Chapter VI

Opinions: Authorities who consider the models in the von Praun Collection to be copies of lost original models by Michelangelo or direct copies of original works by Michelangelo

Ernst Steinmann, in his 1907 *Das Geheimnis der Medicigräber Michelangelos* says: "The scarcity of the Bozzetti (models) in London and Florence which can be attributed to Michelangelo must restrain us from considering the terracottas of the Haehnel Collection as original works of the Master." The models in London to which Steinmann is referring are the wax models from the Gherardini Collection in the Victoria and Albert Museum. Steinmann's judgment has no credible foundation, however, as the numerous models in London from the Gherardini Collection have long since lost their former attribution to Michelangelo. Steinmann, in his 1924 "Michelangelo-Modelle", states that the terracotta models from the von Praun Collection are copies of lost originals by Michelangelo, but he admits to some difficulty in deciding to whom they should be attributed on account of the high quality of the workmanship and its similarity to that of Michelangelo. He also expresses great admiration for the workmanship displayed in the models, but at the same time admits that he never saw the terracottas themselves and that his judgment is based solely on photographs of the models.

Fritz Burger, in his 1907 *Studien zu Michelangelo*, believes the models to be copies of lost originals by Michelangelo and he suggests that the copyist (perhaps Tribolo) may have seen Michelangelo's models when he was working in the Sacristy of the Medici Chapel in Florence. Dr. Burger's theory has

no supporters, and it seems highly unlikely that any copyist would have had access to the Sacristy of the Medici Chapel.

Burger's and Steinmann's opinions concerning the models were completely discounted by Henry Thode's authoritative writings of 1913. Steinmann himself acknowledged Henry Thode's pre-eminence in a subject which so many authorities on Michelangelo have ignored, primarily because of its specialized nature and the personal examinations and studies required of this form of Michelangelo's remarkable creative ability. As Steinmann wrote in his 1924 article on models by Michelangelo:

"In the sixth volume of the critical supplements (which can never be praised enough) to his work on Michelangelo, Thode has put together at least a part of the terracottas which have been ascribed to Michelangelo in the past centuries."

A.E. Brinckmann, in his one-page article titled "Terrakotten Michelangelos (?)" published in 1925, considers the models in the Haehnel Collection to be miserable 16th century copies of Michelangelo's powerful artistic style. He gives no reasons for his opinion, however, except to state that the only authentic models by Michelangelo are to be found in the Casa Buonarroti, Florence, and in the Gherardini Collection of the Victoria and Albert Museum. As in the case of Steinmann he did not see the originals themselves and bases his 1925 judgment solely on the forty photographic plates published by Meier-Graefe in the previous year.

Brinckmann's negative opinion of 1925 is perhaps due to the fact that two years previously he had published (*Barock-Bozzetti*, 1923, Vol. I, pp. 28-39) what he considered to be a complete list of the few surviving authentic models by Michelangelo, and this list did not include the models in the Haehnel Collection. Brinckmann has erroneously stated that a clay model in the Musée Bonat, Bayonne, France, was an original model by Michelangelo ("Belvedere", XI, 1927, p. 155) whereas it is actually a copy, and as already stated the wax sketches from the Gherardini Collection in the Victoria and Albert Museum, which were accepted by him in 1923 and again in 1925 as being by the hand of Michelangelo, have since that time definitely lost that attribution. As in the case of Brinckmann's article "Terrakotten Michelangelos (?)", because of possible loss of prestige, it is a human and perhaps understandable failing of art authorities that once an authority gives his opinion as to the genuiness or non-genuiness of a piece of art, seldom, if ever, will he later reverse that opinion, particularly if it has previously appeared in print. With particular reference to Michelangelo models, Ludwig Goldscheider is an exception to the general rule. In his 1957 *Michelangelo's Bozzetti for Statues in the Medici Chapel* he says that all the models in the Haehnel Collection are copies, whereas five years later in his 1962 publication *A Survey of Michelangelo's Models in Wax and Clay* he shows such nobility of character that he reverses his previously printed opinion. One aspect to be derived from Goldscheider's 1962 authentication should be commented on; if in the Haehnel-von Praun Collection there are, as Goldscheider believes, at least six models which are from the hand of Michelangelo, then it cannot be said with certainty that none of the other models in the Collection merits the same authentic certification—if even just one model is acceptable, then there is strong indication that all or a majority can be accepted, especially as all models in the Collection have the same remarkable provenance.

With reference to the Haehnel Collection, in correspondence dated May 14, 1962, with the author of this volume, the art historian Dr. Hans Huth, then head of the Renaissance Department of The Art Institute of Chicago, wrote:

"I would say that opinions of Messrs. Steinmann and Burger would be of no great importance. Brinckmann's opinion would seem valuable only if he had seen the originals. I have, by the way, known all three men."

The only small model that Bernard Berenson accepted as being by the hand of Michelangelo, is the dark red wax model for "The Young Boboli Giant" from the Gherardini Collection in the Victoria and Albert Museum, but most authorities of today call it a copy. Sir John Pope-Hennessy says, however, that the balance of probability is that it is by Michelangelo. This 6½ inch high wax model has been varnished and its surface is blotchy and discoloured. Broken parts of it have been repaired. Berenson does not refer to the Haehnel-von Praun Collection of models by Michelangelo and it is very doubtful that he ever saw it.

Charles de Tolnay, the excellent and very authoritative writer of a number of volumes on Michelangelo, in his *The Medici Chapel*, Vol. III, 1948, note 9, p. 155, states in a two-line reference that the models in the Haehnel Collection are copies, but makes no other comment except to quote Steinmann (*Geheimnis*, Leipzig, 1907, p. 83) as the basis for his opinion.

It is astonishing how carelessly art authorities have dealt with models by

Michelangelo, not excluding even those very few art historians who have a thorough knowledge of the many other aspects of Michelangelo's remarkable creative ability. As an example of this unconcern, de Tolnay, in note 8, p. 155 of his *The Medici Chapel*, states:

"Terracotta Models of the Allegories, mid-sixteenth century, Formerly Collection Ruland, Weimar, later Collection Percy Strauss, New York, Cf. Thode, Kr. U., i, p. 486, and Steinmann, *Geheimnis*, p. 85 (illus.)."

The one and only model by Michelangelo that was in the Percy Strauss Collection in New York was the model of the "Day" and this is now in the Museum of Fine Arts in Houston, Texas, as part of a substantial donation of art by Percy Strauss and his wife to that museum. The small model of the "Day" (twelve and one-half inches long) in Houston comes from the von Praun Collection and it was one of the models from the Haehnel Collection which were sold at Christie's in 1938. The statuette of a "Nude Youth" (Fig. 159), in the Casa Buonarroti, which de Tolnay discusses at great length in his Vol. 1, fig. 286, on Michelangelo, he identifies as "terracotta" whereas it is quite obviously made of wax. A further example of what appears to be de Tolnay's disinterest in researching models directly relating to Michelangelo's works is found in note 7, p. 155 of his *The Medici Chapel*, in which he says that the model of the "Night" from the Tribolo series is now in the Victoria and Albert Museum, and that this model was in the mid-sixteenth century the property of Vasari and preserved in his house in Arrezzo. De Tolnay is referring to a larger, rather than small sized, terracotta statuette of the "Dawn" (eighteen inches long) which was purchased by the Victoria and Albert Museum from the Gherardini Collection, and

mistakenly describes the statuette as a copy of the "Night". De Tolnay also assumes that it formed part of a set of four medium-sized terracotta copies (twenty-four inches long) of the four "Phases of the Day" in the Medici Chapel, stated by Vasari to have been made by Tribolo (an early student of Michelangelo), of which the "Dawn", the "Day" and the "Evening" are now in the Museo Nazionale, Florence. It should be noted that this last mistake was not made by Thode (*Michelangelo*, IV, Berlin, 1908, p. 485) and that he says the aforesaid model of the "Dawn" in the Victoria and Albert Museum (from the Gherardini Collection) cannot be ascribed to a known hand.

Until de Tolnay's appointment in 1962 as Director of the Casa Buonarroti in Florence, he believed that there existed in the world only two small models (Figs. 7 and 10) which were actually by the hand of Michelangelo, in addition to the full-scale model (Fig. 134) for the "River God" (in the Casa Buonarroti since its removal from the Florence Accademia in 1965). This large model has been generally accepted as being by Michelangelo only within the past sixty-five years; it had previously been attributed to Ammanati. De Tolnay's opinion on the Haehnel-von Praun Collection is based on Ernest Steinmann's, which is no longer considered reliable. Steinmann was a very poor authority on Michelangelo's models—he reproduced in *Geheimnis der Medicigräber Michelangelo* as works of the Master, the models in Edinburgh which are now considered to be fakes, and a number of others which are also definitely false.

It appears that since de Tolnay's appointment as Director of the Casa Buonarroti he has become more expansive and now believes the authenticity of at least six small models, all in the Casa Buonarroti, one of which is a crucifix in wood (Fig. 172) which is approximately five inches high. The 1970 catalogue of the Casa Buonarroti Museum classifies the six small models as being by Michelangelo with an additional three models described as being only attributed to him. It should be noted, however, that one of the three models (Fig. 159) attributed to Michelangelo in the catalogue has in the past been classified by de Tolnay (see Addendum) as an authentic model by Michelangelo.

John Pope-Hennessy, one of today's finest art historians, in his *Catalogue of Italian Sculpture in the Victoria and Albert Museum,* p. 426, Vol. 2, says that the model for the right arm of Christ in the "Pietà" in St. Peter's, Rome, and the model for the right hand of "Moses" (both from the von Praun Collection and both now in the Victoria and Albert Museum) are casts from reduced versions of the "Pietà" and the "Moses", and were there no reason to suppose that they came from the von Praun Collection a more recent origin might be presumed. He further states that the terracotta models in the Victoria and Albert Museum for the "Dawn" and for the "Night" (formerly in the Haehnel-von Praun Collection) are derived from the Medici Tombs, modelled directly, or from bronzes or other reductions, and that they possibly date from the sixteenth century.

There are four small models from the von Praun Collection, as well as the plaquette, "Hercules and Atlas", which Henry Thode doubted were made by the hand of Michelangelo ("Michelangelos Tonmodelle aus der Haehnel'schen Sammlung"). These four models were "The Right Hand of Moses", (Fig. 108), now in the Victoria and Albert Museum; "A Left Foot" (Fig. 56); "A Slender Right Leg" (Fig. 131), and "A Slender Left Leg (Fig. 140), both of which Thode considered to have been made for a cruci-

fix. The two last-named models are now in the Vancouver Collection. With regard to the plaquette (Fig. 168), Thode says:

"I cannot believe that a plaque in terracotta which is rounded at the top and which shows two nude men of a Herculean stature, holding a great ball with violent effort and surrounded by garments, also comes from Michelangelo. The muscles are too strong and too unpleasant — exaggerated in the manner of Bandinelli. Burger is reminded of the sketch of Atlas bearing the world that Michelangelo made for Frederico Ginori, yet he showed there Atlas bearing the world, whereas here is shown Hercules taking the world over from Atlas (if this is shown at all) and the sketch was made for a model which cannot be said for the terracotta."

Professor George Lehnert in his 1913 opinion on the Haehnel Collection, *Expert Opinion on Models by Michelangelo,* ascribed the possible use of casts to far too many models in the Collection and failed to note that where clay models by Michelangelo were to be fired and turned into terracotta, it was in most cases simply a matter of slicing a clay model, while in its leather-hard state, into halves or even into several parts for hollowing-out purposes. When the two halves or parts are joined together prior to firing, it is normal for a faint seam to be detectable in many cases after the firing, as in the case of a number of the hollow models in the Haehnel-von Praun Collection. It is to be noted, however, that Thode did not make the same error as did Lehnert with regard to the use of casts, and where he detected faint seams in the models, he stated in his 1913 article:

"The models are scrupulously built expressions out of a genuine form (double form of front and back halves pressed against each other, compare the seams still recognizable at No. 21). The openings to be found repeatedly in the back served the purpose to avoid, if possible, changes during the processes of burning, when the clay may have been contracted."

Authorities who consider the models of the von Praun Collection to be by the hand of Michelangelo

To some Michelangelo critics the hall-mark of authority as to whether or not a model was actually created by the hand of Michelangelo is the re-worked surface of a wax model (Figs. 4 and 159), or the corroded surface of a terrasecca model (Figs. 7 and 10), which gives them a roughly-finished and in some cases broken appearance. On the other hand, the well preserved terracotta models by Michelangelo have been regarded by some of these critics as copies because they do not have the surface texture that they consider should be evident in original models. It should be noted that where a critic believes that there are only a very few models by the hand of Michelangelo existing today, this reasoning cannot be justified due to the lack of what he would have considered to be authentic terracotta models with which to make a comparison. The wax and terrasecca models by Michelangelo have deteriorated to a marked degree, due to climate and temperature changes, since they were made. The terracotta models by Michelangelo, however, do not seem to have been affected by the passage of time to any great extent. It should therefore be obvious that it is actually easier to establish the authenticity of a terracotta model by Michelangelo than one made by him in wax or in terrasecca.

Michelangelo's biographer Herman Grimm (*Leben Michelangelos*, 1879, Vol. I, p. 488, and Vol. II, pp. 552 and 553) made an intensive study of the Haehnel-von Praun Collection of models and came to the conclusion that they were authentic. Julius Grosse, in his work, *Ernst Julius Haehnel's Literary Relics*, 1893, says on p. 60 that the famous models of the "Phases of the Day" are the original models by the hand of Michelangelo and that the figure of the "Evening" is missing. Carl von Lützow, writing in 1876, regarded the three models of the "Phases of the Day" to be genuine and said:

"The treatment of these sketches carries in all parts the stamp of originality. Nothing can be found therein which would suggest the nervous accuracy of a student or a copyist, or the calculated arbitrariness of a forger. It is the first incommunicable pouring-out of the imagination of the Great Master.

"Michelangelo made only small sketches (not medium sized models) and then he went directly to work on the marble block without the aid of any further auxillary models."

Henry Thode, writing in 1913, (*Michelangelo*, VI, Berlin) on the Collection after having carefully examined the individual models over a considerable period of time, was in a position to know and then deny Burger's opinion, as well as that of Steinmann, both published in 1907. As already stated, the latter's was based solely on the photography of that time and was the quoted reference basis of de Tolnay's opinion in 1948 (*The Medici Chapel*, Vol. III, p. 155, note 9).

It was not until 1913 when, after a lengthy study and after overcoming a preconceived doubt which had been perhaps influenced by Burger's negative opinion of 1907, that Henry Thode came to the strong conviction that most of the models in the Haehnel Collection were by the hand of Michelangelo and by no other hand—Burger thought that some may have been by Tribolo.

Henry Thode in his "Michelangelos Tonmodelle aus der Haehnel'schen Sammlung", wrote with regard to the models in the Haehnel Collection:

"A thorough and repeated examination of the models that have kindly been put at my disposal by their present owners, Fräulein Anna Haehnel and Frau Elise Walter Haehnel in Dresden, has convinced me that we see in most of them genuine studies from the Master's hand, and being genuine they are of great importance and very valuable, although in the beginning one may not have the courage to believe their genuineness with regard to the fact that only a very few of Michelangelo's models have been preserved. Not only their manifold particularities and, as far as they are preparatory work for well known statues, differences from these exclude for my part any doubt, but even more so and in a very decisive manner, also the singular character, full of vigour, the incomparable knowledge of the human body, the intensity of the view, the mighty feeling for the form as well as the masterful execution. It is for me out of the question to speak of copies here where each singular form is directly felt up into the smoothest, most unnoticeable swellings, and yet the structure of the organic whole is completely uniform. Nobody who copies—Burger thinks of Tribolo—would be able to do so with such a combination of greatness and fineness and with such a conclusive authority on life's expression. One can feel the finger of the creator as he animates the clay with the slightest pressure, and one can feel with such an excitement and such a delight, as it is only possible with the creation of one of the greatest artists.

"The above, however, is a judgment based merely on sentiments that are subjective and which can therefore not be regarded in most cases as conclusive, although in reality such a jugment is in many questions of art's history decisive in the end; and if other positive proof cannot be found, one is allowed to build an argument based on their origin, although this may not be a strong one. The well known art connoisseur Paul von Praun (1548-1616) who lived in Bologna and started his art collection in 1576, was advised in his art purchases in that city by the best artists. Since 1616 his collection was the pride of Nuremberg as the 'Art Cabinet' famous under his name. However, it is not known from whom he bought the models, but at the time this happened—not too long a time after the death of Michelangelo—he was well in a position to learn of their origin and genuineness with the help of his artist friends. The selectivity and the fame of his collection, for which he managed to acquire amongst other objects a great number of the famous drawings which Vasari had collected, shows with what great care he acted.

"It may further be noted that after Paul von Praun's death no further purchases have been made for his 'Art Cabinet', which means that the models must have been acquired all by himself."

Professor George Lehnert was of the opinion that the models in the Haehnel Collection were creations of the Master or alternatively, where a seam in the clay is detectable, they are the first and sole copies of original wax models made by him. He says:

"The overall style, the movement, the treatment of the skin, certain peculiarities like the typical shape of the hands, the fingers and fingernails, all these facts make it clear that these models are the works of Michelangelo. This is especially significant with respect to the three main, the 'Day', the 'Night' and the 'Dawn'.

"It is impossible to think that these models, attributed to Michelangelo, were made by someone else. These models coincide in their particular peculiarities and in their overall expression, that they are the works of the Great Master. Besides those marked points in which they differ from other models, it is definitely established that they are working models of the master sculptor. These deviations make it very clear that these models were the actual working models which Michelangelo used to create his beautiful monumental works in statuary. A faker who might have gone out of his way to make slight changes in the models, in order to make them appear as if they were study models of the Master, usually would have a rude awakening. That is to say, a faker would have made such gross errors in the models that an art connoisseur would have detected the fake right away. These deviations in the here-mentioned models which the Master used for his final monuments, are proof that they are the real and genuine models."

In 1924 Meier-Graefe published a very large portfolio of forty photographic engravings of the models in the Haehnel Collection, and he was convinced of the genuineness of the Collection. Ludwig Goldscheider, who has made the study of Michelangelo one of the specialities of his distinguished career as an art historian and author, went to Canada from Britain in 1962 for the specific purpose of examining the Canadian Collection of Michelangelo models. Goldscheider, who undoubtedly has a far greater knowledge of models by Michelangelo than any other of the all-too-few living experts on Michelangelo's works, is of the opinion that there are at least six models in the Vancouver Collection by the hand of the great Master—he is silent with respect to eleven models which compose the balance of the Collection. The six models by Michelangelo in the Vancouver Collection are well illustrated and thoroughly discussed in his book, *A Survey of Michelangelo's Models in Wax and Clay*, published by The Phaidon Press in 1962. According to Goldscheider, out of the fifteen to eighteen models by Michelangelo extant in the world, approximately one-third (six) are in the Canadian Collection.

In the "Commentary" of the catalogue of the Canadian Collection of models by Michelangelo, when six of the models were privately exhibited in Montreal in 1963, Ludwig Goldscheider says:

"There are two reasons why so few of Michelangelo's models have come down to us. One is that such sketches in wax and clay perish easily, the other that Michelangelo himself destroyed many of them. We know that in 1518, when he gave up his house in Rome, all the cartoons and drawings which were still there, were burned by his orders and that a few days before his death he asked that all 'sketches' in the house should be destroyed. This was carried out and

only three cartoons and a number of architectural designs escaped destruction. One can safely assume that his hatred of all sketches did not exclude the models in clay and wax. Why did Michelangelo act in such a manner? Was it his desire that other artists should not learn his methods from his sketches? We find the answer in Vasari (VII, 270): 'I know that shortly before his death Michelangelo burned a great number of his drawings, models, and cartoons (*disegni, schizzi, e cartoni*), so that none might see how hard he had worked and in which ways he had tried out his genius.'

"But it is, of course, against reason to assume that all the original models are lost and only copies preserved. The originals have always been known as such by tradition, and good care was taken to save them from destruction.

"Some thirty years ago Michelangelo's finest drawings were always regarded with suspicion, and if their style was in some way unusual they were called 'copies'. But this pedantic and contractive method is now discredited, owing to the work of Johannes Wilde, Barocchi, and other students. Michelangelo research has returned in a certain degree to Thode's opinions so far as the drawings are concerned, but his attitude towards the models has not yet been vindicated.

"There is no definite consensus about the models. Forty years ago the large terracotta model of a 'River God' in the Florence Accademia was not accepted as an original by C. Frey and A.E. Popp, the best 'Michelangelo experts' of their time. Frey called it 'too poor in quality'. Popp attributed it to Ammanati. Today, however, there is no one who would doubt the authenticity of this grand model. On the other hand, the small wax model for a 'River God' (in the British Museum) is still doubted. Not by Wilde, who accepts it as one of the only two genuine models in England, but by Charles de Tolnay, who considers it as 'weak in execution and not in the style of Michelangelo'. Neither does he regard as genuine a particularly fine, though not softly modelled terracotta torso in the Casa Buonarroti. 'This model', he says, 'which is of high quality, does not show the texture of the original models of Michelangelo'. As Tolnay's monumental work is the greatest contribution to Michelangelo literature since the days of Justi and Thode, his judgments have an overpowering influence even in cases where they can be contested.

"If the provenance of a model can be traced as far back as the time of the late Renaissance, one should always hesitate to deny the authenticity of such a piece. There are only two ancient collections of wax and clay sketches by Michelangelo—the Paul von Praun Collection in Bologna and the Buonarroti Collection in Florence. Some of the models there are originals, others are copies produced by the 'garzoni de Michelangelo'. The Buonarroti Collection owns now six genuine models—another two were sold and belong to the British Museum. The models, which were in the von Praun Collection between 1590 and 1598, were catalogued in 1913 by Thode when they belonged to the Haehnel heirs in Dresden. His list enumerates thirty-three pieces, of which, I believe, at least six are authentic. They are now in the Vancouver Collection."

The von Praun Collection was in total, or at least in part, composed of models that are authentic according to the convictions of many famous art authorities of the past. A list of authorities would include Herman Grimm, writing in 1879 (*Leben Michelangelos*) and in 1880 (*Jahrbuch der Königlichen Preussischen Kunstsammlungen*); Meier-Graefe, in a special publication along with a very large volume of forty photo-engravings published in Berlin in 1924 under the title *Michelangelo. Die Terrakotten aus der Sammlung Haehnel*, and such other notable art critics as Avenarius, Pfister, Springer, Gottschewski, Lützow, Hampe; Professor Haehnel, of course, who wrote several articles on the subject, and the art historian, Christophe Theophile Murr, the cataloguer of the von Praun Collection. All these art authorities are united in their opinion that the terracotta models in the Haehnel-von Praun Collection, or at least certain specified parts of it, are by the hand of Michelangelo. Kurt Pfister in his "Die Terrakotten Michelangelos" article of 1924 stated:

"At least a considerable part (of the Haehnel Collection of models) can be expected to have been created by Michelangelo's own hand. Not only is the origin of the works first class; Paul von Praun acquired the Collection in 1598 in Bologna probably from Vasari's heirs and at a time close to the death of Michelangelo. Also the conception and the execution speak quite against the assumption that this is the work of students for the purpose of study or forgery. The fragments not only show the anatomical details to be copied and carried out by Michelangelo in marble, but individual ones also show the rhythmic motives which portray the genius-like inspiration of the moulder and which of necessity often lose some of their originality in the completed marble work."

Generally speaking, besides Professor Goldscheider, the most authoritative of all the writers on models by Michelangelo is Henry Thode, a renowned art historian, Professor at Heidelberg, and author of six books and numerous articles on the Renaissance and on Michelangelo in particular.

A Sculptor's Tools, typical of those used by Michelangelo for sculpturing in marble, from the reliefs on the marble tomb of the sculptor Andrea Bregno, 1506—Rome, Santa Maria sopra Minerva.

Additional reasons why the great majority of the models in the von Praun Collection are original models by the hand of Michelangelo

If all the models in the von Praun Collection are copies of lost original models by Michelangelo and are not therefore directly from the Master's hand, it is very surprising that not one of these supposed original models by Michelangelo exists today to substantiate this theory, which was first compounded by Burger and Steinmann in 1907. The theory was completely discounted by Thode in 1913, by Meier-Graefe in 1924 and by Goldscheider in 1962. According to Thode, the majority of the terracotta models are of such perfection that they could only have been created by one of the greatest of artists—Michelangelo himself—and not by a copyist of his original models.

It is also surprising that so few of Michelangelo's small models have survived to this day (only those shown in Figs. 7 and 10, according to de Tolnay's opinion not too long before his appointment as Director of the Casa Buonarroti), especially in view of the esteem in which they were held in Michelangelo's own day and subsequently. With the exception of the terracotta model in the British Museum (Fig. 171), it is indeed significant that outside of the von Praun Collection no other similar models of terracotta have ever changed hands in any art dealings of the past. It is not unreasonable to suppose that more than two models have survived, and that to those few that are today generally considered as genuine, should be added all, or at least a large percentage, of the forty models originally in the von Praun Collection, a collection formed shortly after the death of Michelangelo and kept

intact for the most part until the Christie's sale of 1938. Can as much be said with respect to the history and the authenticity of other models by Michelangelo? Sir Eric Maclagan in his *Burlington Magazine* article of 1924 (Vol. XLIV) states on p. 15: "The models in the Casa Buonarroti are not very easy to study, and so far as I know no catalogue of them, except the list by Dr. Thode, has ever been published." A number of the models in the von Praun Collection have a small hole in them in order that they could be hung by a string and studied by Michelangelo from all angles. If these models were copies of the original statues or even of lost original models, it is very doubtful that the copyist would have placed these holes in them.

The clay models from the von Praun Collection show distinct differences in tone and colour which varies from a light yellow, to ochre and to a reddish dark brown. The reason for the colour variation is that the models were created at different times and at different places. If the owner of an original Michelangelo model had wished to produce copies in order to sell them to art dealers, he would have produced the copies at the same time and in the same clay material, and the then fired objects would all have been of the same colour. Such is not the case, however, with the models from the von Praun Collection.

It should not be forgotten that Paul von Praun was a contemporary of Michelangelo (he was sixteen when Michelangelo died) and that he started his collection in Bologna, which was one of the principal centres of art in Italy at that time. Praun, being wealthy and well educated, was in a favourable position to be advised by the best artists of the day, such as his close friend the sculptor Giovanni da Bologna (a former student of Michelangelo's), and undoubtedly would have known the difference between a copy and an original model by Michelangelo. Von Praun was one of the greatest art collectors of his day and he was, in fact, an advisor in art to kings and to many of the nobility of his time.

If anybody had been desirous of faking a model by Michelangelo, it is almost certain that he would have faked a complete model, such as one of the "Phases of the Day". It is most unlikely that anyone would have faked a study of an individual part of the proposed complete statue, as for example, "the right hand of 'Dawn" (Fig. 17). Studies in wax and clay of individual parts of the human body not only fit into the normal pattern of Michelangelo's work method, but there also exists a similar pattern or trend in drawings by the Great Master.

Professor Lehnert speaks of deviations between the models and the final finished statuary. In this category he includes the "Mask" and the "Owl" of the "Night" in the von Praun Collection which, he points out, differ substantially in the finished marble. He remarks on the fact that the left hand of "Giuliano" in clay holds an article other than the rod of the statue, and that the clay arm of "Christ" is resting on a support other than that shown in the marble statue of the "Pietà". The model of the "Day" wins Lehnert's support primarily because its face and head are perfectly executed, whereas the face and head of the marble statue were left unfinished. The same circumstance applies in the case of the model of the "Night", as

its left hand and lower arm are perfectly executed, but left only as a stump of rough-hewn marble in the Medici Chapel figure. Contemporary sources state that the Master chipped away and completely ruined the left arm of the marble "Night" in his attempt to alter it.

The painting "Sight", by Jan Brueghel the "Elder" now in the Prado Museum dated ca. 1617, shows four small models by Michelangelo (Fig. 144). Two of these models are for the "Night" and for the "Dawn", while the other two are models for the two slaves for the "Julius Monument", namely the "Dying Captive" and the "Heroic Captive". It is only in the Paul von Praun Collection that these four models are recorded (Murr's Catalogue, p. 241) as having existed together in one collection, and therefore there is every reason to believe that these four models are the original inspiration for the inclusion of four Michelangelo models in the Brueghel painting. It is very possible that the four models in the painting were taken from drawings of the four models in the von Praun Collection, which were done during the course of Brueghel's short visit to Italy in 1596—after moving early in his life to Antwerp, he never left there except for that trip to Italy. The painting is one of a series of five panels depicting imaginary landscapes, architecture, and interiors with collections of paintings by Rubens and other artists, and with sculptures and busts, in addition to numerous other man-made objects which Brueghel was fond of portraying so as to display his skill and virtuosity in a single painting or series of paintings.

There is every indication that Rubens' three sketches (Fig. 62) after Michelangelo's "Night", presently in The Hague, were not drawings of the marble figure in the Medici Chapel and that the model for the "Night" from the von Praun Collection and now in the Victoria and Albert Museum was the actual model from which Rubens made the sketches. There also exists the possibility that von Praun, who lived at the time of Michelangelo and Tintoretto and who also possessed drawings and paintings by Michelangelo and by Tintoretto, may have purchased some of his Michelangelo models directly from Tintoretto, as the latter is known to have possessed a number of small original Michelangelo models, among them a clay sketch of "Hercules and Cacus". The story of Antonio Mini and his possession of two large boxes full of terracotta models by Michelangelo is also well-known. When Mini died in France, all his Michelangelo treasures disappeared except for a few models which Leonardo da Vinci's friend, Rustici, brought back to Florence. Perhaps these few models found their way into the von Praun Collection which was formed about this time (see reference to the Canadian Collection, p. 223 of the 4th edition of the volume, *Michelangelo: Paintings, Sculptures, Architecture,* by Goldscheider).

As has already been pointed out, both the Murr Catalogue of the von Praun Collection and Henry Thode state that Paul von Praun bought in Bologna (directly from the heir and nephew of Vasari) the balance of the Vasari Collection of drawings which the heir had brought from Rome to Bologna at the end of the sixteenth century.

Vasari, who was a contemporary of von Praun, owned small models by Michelangelo (clay sketches for the head and the arms of "Cosmas") and as reported by Murr and Thode many drawings, and very possibly a number of paintings by the great masters in the Vasari Collection, found their way into the von Praun Collection. It is therefore conceivable that one or more of the clay models by Michelangelo in the von Praun Collection were originally in the Vasari Collection.

Michelangelo left Florence before he completed the Medici Chapel monuments. The fact that the face of the figure in the model of the "Day" (now in the Houston Museum) is complete, as is its head of the antique Herculean-type, proves that the small clay model is older than the marble figure in the Chapel. According to Henry Thode, the stupendous head of the "Day" by itself is sufficient to prove the genuineness of the von Praun model, as well as of all the others which are so very similar in their execution. Thode further states that: "...none of Michelangelo's imitators, even the most endowed, would have been able to create anything like it; one has only to compare statues of Raffaele da Montelupo or of Montorsoli, or even of Giovanni da Bologna." Additional proof of authenticity is the fact that the left hand of the marble figure of the "Night" in the Medici Chapel is partially shortened and has been left incomplete by Michelangelo, whereas the lovely terracotta model of the "Night", now in the Victoria and Albert Museum, shows a left hand which is complete in all respects.

On April 20th, 1562, Allessandro Vittorio, the sculptor and former student of Michelangelo, is reported to have bought the small clay model for "The Left Foot of Day" by Michelangelo. It is very unlikely that this famous sculptor would have bought a falsification. Herman Grimm (*Leben Michelangelos,* 1879, Vol. 2, pp. 552 and 553) was of the strong opinion that the terracotta model for the left foot of "Day" in the Haehnel-von Praun Collection was the same model that Vittorio had previously purchased from the Bologna art dealer, Nicolo Zolfino, for three Venetian skudi.

In his 1924 publication on the terracottas from the Haehnel Collection, Professor Julius Meier-Graefe says:

"Today it would be difficult for anyone with a well-founded veneration for Michelangelo to imagine that the Titan who created the collossi of the Medici Tombs being contented with diminutive versions of his vision. Yet even the work of a Michelangelo probably begins with modest dimensions. Just as there were drawings for the sublime works of San Lorenzo—drawings which spell out in detail what is to our imagination an insoluble complex—there were small-scale models, auxiliary studies, fragile details. It may be painful for the veneration, which has expanded into the mythical, to be reminded of these paths of creation to the finished work."

Perhaps one of the reasons why certain art historians have rejected some or all of the Michelangelo models from the von Praun Collection and many or all of them in the Casa Buonarroti Collection (see Addendum)

is that they are still overawed by the sublimity and energy of Michelangelo—a genius above all other geniuses. In his own day he was considered divine. Vasari wrote in his *Lives of the Artists*:

"This master, as I said in the beginning, was certainly sent by God as an example of what an artist could be. I, who can thank God for unusual happiness, count it among the greatest of my blessings that I was born while Michelangelo still lived, was found worthy to have him for my Master, and was accepted as his trusted friend."

The hero worship expressed by Vasari has been continued over the centuries. To conceive of Michelangelo working on difficult details of his monumental marble statues, like a virtuoso practising scales on the piano, disturbs the image. Nevertheless, his genius is in no way diminished by the admission that he also used his ingenuity.

Bronze Bust—Portrait Of Michelangelo taken from the death mask—by Daniele da Volterra.

135

Chapter VII

The importance of the models by Michelangelo in the von Praun Collection

They show Michelangelo's work method

When one looks at Michelangelo's paintings and sculptures, in the museums of Florence, London and Paris, and in many Florentine and Roman chapels and churches, or if one studies reproductions of his works, the beauty and the power inherent in them becomes very apparent.

A wealth of literature has been published on the history of Michelangelo's sculptures, paintings and drawings, and of the forces that motivated the Master, but with the exception of Ludwig Goldscheider's *A Survey of Michelangelo's Models in Wax and Clay,* there is no volume which can fully enlighten us on the methods used by Michelangelo in creating his masterpieces. For example, how did Michelangelo design and paint the three or four hundred figures in his "Last Judgment" fresco? It does not seem plausible that he used living models; it is more probable that he used many wax and clay models for the Herculean male and female figures, some of whom swarm up to Heaven, while others fall into the depths of Hades. Not only had Michelangelo the task of preparing hundreds of cartoons for this fresco, but he must also have made a great many drawings and models for many of the single figures or their parts in these cartoons.

Once fired, clay is virtually indestructible — consequently the surviving Michelangelo terracotta models formerly in the von Praun Collection have come down to us in an unaltered and almost perfect condition. These models, with their known history, are among our chief sources of information on one of the work methods used by that great artist, a man of such genius that to this day he towers over all others in the world of art.

Vasari in the "Introduction to Sculpture" of his *Lives of the Most Eminent Painters . . .,* published in 1550, stated:

"When sculptors wish to work on a marble statue they usually make first what they call 'a model' for it, which is a guide-pattern, about half a braccio high (approximately eleven and a half inches), sometimes less or more, just as it suits them; and they make it in clay, or wax, or stucco. Such a model shows, in accordance with dimensions of the block quarried for the statue, the attitude and the proportions of the figure.

"If he wants to make his model in clay, he works exactly as with wax, but there will be no armature of wood or iron because this would cause the clay to crack or split. To avoid cracking, the clay model has to be kept covered with a wet cloth until it is finished."

Cellini in his *Due Trattati dell' Orificeria e della Scultura* commented:

"When you have made a satisfactory model you draw the principal views of your statue on the stone; and mind it be well drawn, for if not you may miscut your block. The best method I ever saw was that which Michelangelo used, which is to draw the front view and then carve around it, as if you wanted to make a relief, and then to cut deeper and more freely.

"To succeed with a figure in marble the art requires a good craftsman first to set up a little model about two palms high (about eight inches). In this model he carefully thinks out the pose, making his figure draped or nude, as the case may be. After this he makes a second model much more carefully than the smaller."

The drawings made by Michelangelo in preparation for his marble sculpture and his fresco paintings are quite well known. Michelangelo's plastic sketches, however, are at present practically unknown, although these models throw much more light on the Master's method of creation than do his sketches on paper. The latter, in fact, only served to fix Michelangelo's first idea.

The Michelangelo models in the von Praun Collection are of great importance as they are the means whereby we are shown how Michelangelo as a sculptor went from drawing to clay, and from clay to marble. They demonstrate to us how his monumental works were made, first in the artist's mind and then in their execution; thus we gain an understanding of the Master's working methods.

Goldscheider, in his *Survey,* describes very well the genesis of a statue in the Medici Chapel.

Firstly, he shows a small ink drawing by Michelangelo, which simply indicates the outlines of a marble block and its measurements. Many such sketches were sent by the Master to the stone masons who quarried blocks of marble for him in Carrara.

Secondly, he shows a spirited drawing presenting two views of a reclining figure, such as for the "Night". This second drawing helps us to see how Michelangelo's imagination had begun to work on the stone, which at that time was still a part of the marble rocks of Carrara and not yet quarried by the stone masons.

Thirdly, he shows a very small, rather sketchy plastic model (e.g., Fig. 135) for the statue the Master had in mind.

Fourthly, he shows a more finished small model in wax or clay. We thus see that the artist, in the last two steps of his work method, has moved away from his two-dimensional sketches on paper and that his vision has gained plasticity.

Fifthly, Goldscheider shows that Michelangelo also made plastic models for parts of the human body, and he juxtaposes these models with detailed photographs of the same parts in the finished marble sculptures.

As already stated, Michelangelo used some of his models over a number of years in many different positions, and often a model used in one position was used in reverse or in "mirror image" in another position. Professor Goldscheider illustrates this work method of Michelangelo's very clearly in his *Survey.*

In Meier-Graefe's publication of 1924 he states that Michelangelo, in his attempt to realize sculptural conceptions with which his mind might never again be presented, had particular reasons for being concerned about the preservation of his models, especially during the lengthy periods between the conception and completion of his finished marbles. When the work in San Lorenzo was interrupted in 1527 after the Medici had been driven out of Florence, and no outward sign was permitted which might be a reminder of the despised commissioners of the Medici Tombs, the terracotta models might well have served as an intended means of preservation of what was eventually to be the form of the finished statuary. Meier-Graefe surmises that Michelangelo may have had the terracotta models among his belongings when he fled to Venice, and that he may even have had them in his primitive quarters near San Miniato during the seige of Florence. Meier-Graefe also states:

"Limbs, torsos and heads did not mean the same thing to the Master of the Sistine Chapel as they do to a layman. The arm and the foot were for him not just anatomical details, but rather they were very specific rhythmic motifs which in certain cases retained their special significance as fragments. He stood far above his own age with such conceptions.

"Is there a facial expression for this body? Must it not necessarily lag behind the expression of the limbs? The physiognomy of a sculpture is not to be found in the face."

Pfister in his 1924 article writes:

"What was the purpose of Michelangelo in making such models? Perhaps so that he could see them in front of him, right to the completion of the marble works which often took years; to always see in front of him the source of his inspiration so as to be able to fire that inspiration within himself again and again. Perhaps he took the models with him during his frequent journeys and perhaps he also had the assurance in war-times that if the finished marble works were themselves destroyed, the models at least would survive."

Thode, who in his 1913 writings on the Haehnel Collection made the most exhaustive study of the terracottas of all the researchers, stated as follows with regard to Michelangelo's work method:

"It is further to be noted that in most cases of missing limbs, as Burger correctly mentioned, a later breakup is not the explanation, but that these apparent breaks, as they have been built, were made purposely in the beginning. That such a limitation on single parts of the body has been a special peculiarity of Michelangelo's form study, is proved by many of his sketches, many of which must have been made directly after such models. Moreover, the particularity of those sketches is only explained by the models, so that in it can be found a strong argument for their genuineness. It can escape nobody's notice, that those studies generally have in this characteristic procedure an importance for the knowledge of the master's work method. It is only by these studies that the scrupulous preparatory work for his statues (and paintings), which is re ported by Vasari and Cellini, is brought into a clear light. The conscientious and detailed perfection of the form in the small models is comparable to the diligent execution of his body models in many of his sketches and demands, same as these, an admiration, which the spectator can hardly put into words."

The Michelangelo models from the von Praun Collection are extraordinary both for their power and their delicacy. Many of them show the surface veining and the stretching of the weight-bearing muscles.

According to Ludwig Goldscheider the comparatively few models that survive from Michelangelo's own hand, and even those from his workshop, are momentous for the understanding of his great works in fresco and in marble. They show us, just as much as his many drawings do, ". . . the various ways in which he tried out his genius", to use Vasari's words.

It is impossible to truly understand Michelangelo's works, unless we know and understand their genesis, and therefore a knowledge of his models is essential, as well as of their historical and biographical background.

A Sculptor's Tool (drill), typical of that used by Michelangelo for sculpturing in marble, from the reliefs on the marble tomb of the sculptor Andrea Bregno, 1506—Rome, Santa Maria sopra Minerva.

They demonstrate the direct influence of the "Antique" on Michelangelo

It was not due to having slavishly copied ancient statuary which gave the Italian sculptors of the Renaissance their fertility and life. Their triumph resulted from the fact that classical art was the heritage of the Italians, who were the legitimate successors of the Romans and the Greeks. The Italian School of the fifteenth and sixteenth centuries, with its classical aspirations, assimilated this classical spirit and without forsaking nature made it one of its own. Those works of art by Michelangelo which show the direct influence of the classical spirit are much more than a mere echo of antiquity. Michelangelo served two masters—nature on one hand, antiquity on the other; it was this dual influence which explains much of his achievement. It was from nature that he derived his inspiration—his free and clear vision. He was ever ready to take advantage of the lessons of science and eagerly studied the anatomy of man. It was from the "Antique", however, that Michelangelo derived his beauty of form, his purity of line and his nobility of conception.

Michelangelo's first piece of marble sculpture was made when, as a student under Bertoldo's tutelage in the Medici Gardens at San Marco, he carved the head of a faun which he had copied from an ancient marble. In the main he and his fellow students made drawings after ancient sculptures and engraved gems that were kept in Bertoldo's academy where they were used as studies for anatomy purposes. There are a number of early Michelangelo drawings which are after the "Antique". The Musée Condé at Chantilly has a Michelangelo drawing of a nude female figure, in two attitudes, which is derived from an ancient statue, very possibly of Venus. Until the age of about thirty, Michelangelo as a draftsman was still very much dependent on antique sculpture and he drew from such ancient marbles as the "Apollo Belvedere". One of his ink sketches in the Louvre appears to have been copied from the "Mercury of the Horti Farnesiani" in Rome.

There were many Greek statues or Roman copies of Grecian sculpture which undoubtedly played a part in their influence on Michelangelo, particularly in his formative years. The "Belvedere Torso" was in the possession of the Colonnas in 1430; the "Apollo Belvedere" had been found at the end of the 15th century; in 1501 the "Pasquino" was discovered, and in 1506 one of the most famous of finds, the "Laocoön Group", was unearthed in Nero's Domus Aurea. The "Hercules Farnese", the "Horse Tamers of the Capital", and the "Dying Gaul" are three other late Greek sculptures which Michelangelo very likely saw and studied. Michelangelo was among the first to admire the "Laocoön Group", which was unearthed in his presence, and he is known to have been greatly impressed by the "Belvedere Torso". As evidenced in many of his own works, he learnt a great deal from these two late Hellenistic sculptures.

Many of the terracotta models by Michelangelo in the von Praun Collection point to the fact that Michelangelo took great pains to master in every detail, through careful studies, not only natural forms but also the "Antique" forms. Thode stated that a number of the models he examined in the Haehnel Collection show in a direct, but not in a slavish fashion, work done in the style of the "Antique", especially in imitation of Praxiteles. He further went on to say that he himself was undecided about the authenticity of the models for a long time, until conformities with sketches and statues, made during the Master's youth, justified his opinion that the models were genuine.

The Haehnel-von Praun Collection contained a number of clay models which are studies by Michelangelo after the "Antique" or of a character according to the "Antique", and are directly related to some of the great Greek sculptures that preceded his. It is also apparent that Michelangelo made a practice, particularly in his youth, of reversing antique motifs in his sculpture. With special regard to several models of torsos and limbs, it is only in the Haehnel-von Praun Collection of terracotta models and in certain drawings by Michelangelo, that this relationship of Michelangelo to Greek art can be clearly traced.

The Medici Chapel, Florence. Tomb of Lorenzo de'Medici, Duke of Urbino.

General reasons for the importance of the models

Apart from the Collection in Vancouver, and the model for the "Day" in the Museum of Fine Arts in Houston, there are no other pieces of sculpture by Michelangelo on the North American continent. The Canadian Collection is the largest in the world in number of Michelangelo models, and the finest in terms of fragmentary studies of the human anatomy, with particular reference to the finished statues in the Medici Chapel and to studies after the "Antique". There exists no other comparable private collection. In fact, there are so few Michelangelo models in existence today that there is an increasing awareness that the models in the Vancouver Collection, along with those in the Victoria and Albert Museum and the the model in the Museum in Houston, are of utmost importance to obtain a full appreciation and understanding of the genius of Michelangelo. The entire collection of Michelangelo models in the Praunsche Kabinett was of terracotta and not of terrasecca, and this accounts for the remarkable state of preservation over the past four hundred odd years of the twenty-two models which have survived from the original forty models in the von Praun Collection. It is to be regretted, that of the missing eighteen terracotta Michelangelo models, eleven have been lost since the Christie's sale in 1938 of the Haehnel-von Praun Collection.

Of considerable interest is the fact that no models of single parts of the body by Michelangelo are known, other than those in the Vancouver Collection. Among the public collections in Europe and in America are a great variety of drawings by Michelangelo; of single legs, arms, hands and torsos, used by him in the preparation of his sculpture and paintings. All the drawings for the ceiling of the Sistine Chapel in Rome were burnt in 1518 according to his wishes. In 1529, when Michelangelo's studio in Florence was broken into, four of his models and many of his drawings were stolen. Shortly before his death he asked that all sketches in his house be destroyed, and as previously noted this request was carried out; only three cartoons and a number of architectural designs escaped destruction. It can be assumed that his dislike of leaving his sketches behind him did not exclude his models in wax and clay, and that the personal destruction during his lifetime of many of his models was partly motivated by the fact that he did not want others to know that a number of them were used by him over and over again in various poses required by him in some of his marble sculpture, and in various figures in several of his paintings (e.g., the "Last Judgment"). One of the most justifiable criticisms that Michelangelo himself very likely heard about his artistic ability is that too often the same torso or limb is seen in several of his works, even though in each case it may be twisted or posed in a slightly different manner. These unfortunate losses and the lamentable destruction of Michelangelo's models, and Michelangelo's movements from one place to another (Florence, Bologna, Rome, Ferrara, Carrara) with his models, friable and cumbersome as they were, explain to a large extent why so few models by Michelangelo have survived to this day. The remaining models are infinitely precious, not only because of the insight they provide into Michelangelo's methods, but because of their rarity.

The following words of Henry Thode on the Haehnel-von Praun Collection ("Michelangelos Tonmodelle aus der Haehnel'schen Sammlung") are even more true today, particularly as only twenty-two of the models still survive, than they were when he wrote them in 1913:

"If we consider that the Master himself has destroyed almost all his models in the desire to keep the traces of his work from the eyes of people, we cannot be grateful enough to the miraculous chance that this collection has come into our time."

The Medici Chapel, Florence. Tomb of Giuliano de'Medici, Duke of Nemours.

Addendum

Other extant models

Extant models in addition to those surviving from the Paul von Praun Collection and which are generally considered to be by the hand of Michelangelo

169
Male Statuette, both arms missing —yellowish wax model, in the Casa Buonarroti, Florence, about 1504.

Casa Buonarroti, Florence

1 A "Slave" or a "River God", head missing (Fig. 4). Light brown wax, 9 inches high.

2 Male statuette, right arm missing (Fig. 159). Dark brown wax, 19½ inches high.

3 Allegorical female figure, head missing, (Fig. 7). Terrasecca, 13½ inches high (badly preserved).

4 Victory Group (*Hercules and Cacus*), (Fig. 10). Terrasecca, 16½ inches high (badly preserved and badly restored).

5 Male statuette, both arms missing, (Fig. 169). Yellowish wax, 21½ inches high (badly preserved, right leg has been wrongly restored).

6 Male torso, model for
the *Awakening Slave*,
(Fig. 170). Terrasecca,
8½ inches high.

7 Male torso, (Fig. 9).
Terracotta, 9½ inches high.

8 A "River God", (Fig. 134).
Terrasecca and oakum,
over wood, 70 inches
long (damaged).

British Museum, London

1 A "River God", (Fig. 135).
Brown wax, 5 inches long.

2 Male torso, (Fig. 171).
Terracotta, 11½ inches
high (later painted green
and repaired with wax).

170 Male Torso, model for the *Awakening Slave*—terrasecca
model, in the Casa Buonarroti, Florence, about 1530.

171 Male Torso—terracotta model, in the
British Museum, London, about 1530.

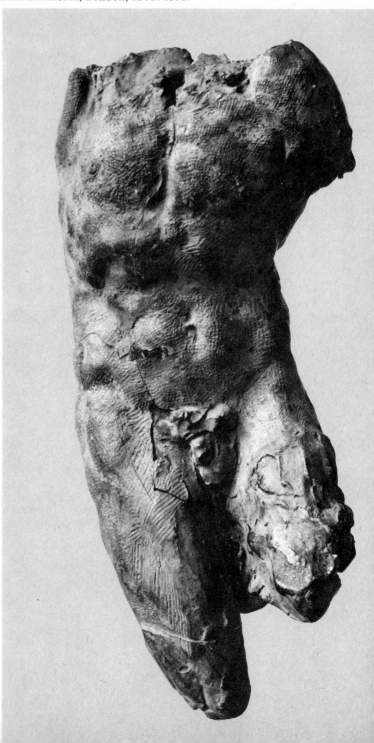

The sculptures of Michelangelo

A listing of Models in the Casa Buonarroti according to the Museum's Catalogue published in December, 1970—Charles de Tolnay—Director

Models by Michelangelo

MODEL FOR A "HERCULES"

(Wax—Fig. 169)

The catalogue's photographic reproduction and the description of the model appears to deny de Tolnay's former identification, wherein he calls the model a "Sketch for David" on p. 165 in *The Complete Work of Michelangelo*. The catalogue also states that the model was repainted in brownish-red, probably to hide the restoration of the feet.

Goldscheider is doubtful as to the authenticity of this model, although considered an original by Thode, Brinkmann and Knapp.

MODEL FOR A "RIVER GOD"

(Wax—Fig. 4)

Accepted by de Tolnay since Goldscheider's authentication.

MODEL FOR *HERCULES AND CACUS*

("Victory Group")

(Terrasecca—Fig. 10)

Before Johannes Wilde's incomplete restoration in 1927 of much of the whole, after he had discovered the lost head, this terrasecca model had previously consisted of two torsos without heads, arms or hands. Prior to about 1962 this was the only model in the Casa Buonarroti completely acceptable to de Tolnay as an original model by Michelangelo —agreeing with Thode, Knapp, Bode and Goldscheider as to its authenticity.

MODEL OF A FEMALE NUDE

(An "Allegorical Female Figure")

(Terrasecca—Fig. 7).

The catalogue states that the model is of terracotta. Maclagan and Goldscheider, however, say that it is made of dried clay (terrasecca).

This model, prior to de Tolnay's authentication, had been accepted by Thode, Bode, Wilde and Goldscheider. It is about the same size as the "Victory Group", of the same material and of a similar technique.

MODEL OF A TORSO OF A "HERMAPHRODITE"

(Terracotta—Fig. 9)

Professor Goldscheider in his *Survey of Michelangelo's Models* believes in the authenticity of this terracotta and, identifying it as a "Male Torso", says: "It is probably one of the models which Michelangelo used for the Last Judgment". Although Charles de Tolnay in his 1970 catalogue of the "Sculptures of Michelangelo" in the Casa Buonarroti lists the model as by the hand of the Great Master, he previously was of a contrary opinion. As noted in Chapter VI of this volume, Goldscheider referring to de Tolnay states:

"Neither does he regard as genuine a particularly fine, though not softly modelled terracotta torso in the Casa Buonarroti . . . This Model", he says, "which is of high quality, does not show the texture of the original models of Michelangelo."

MODEL OF A "CHRIST ON THE CROSS"

(Wood—Fig. 172)

This small model (approx. 5 inches high) was ascribed to Michelangelo by de Tolnay in "Commentari", 1965, as a late work of the Great Master. Henry Thode and Sir Eric Maclagan were not of that opinion. Most writers have failed in the past to even mention this small and incomplete crucifix in wood.

MODEL OF A "RIVER GOD"

(Terrasecca and oakum over wood—Fig. 134)

This is the only extant large-scale model by Michelangelo. It is 70 inches long. De Tolnay agrees with Adolf Gottschewski, Hildebrand, Frida Schottmüller, Wilde and Goldscheider that this is an original large model by Michelangelo. Carl Frey and A. E. Popp, however, have attributed it to Ammanati.

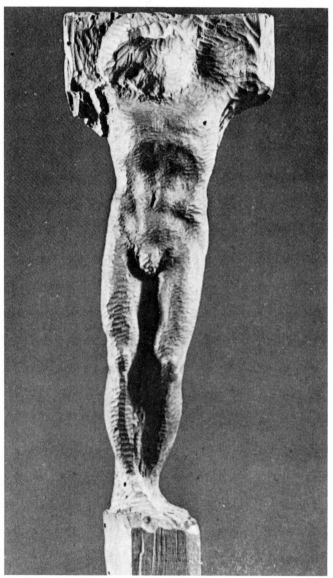

172 *Christ on the Cross*—wooden model, in the Casa Buonarroti, Florence, about 1562.

Models attributed
to Michelangelo

MODEL FOR A *DAVID*

(Wax—Fig. 159)

Once again the catalogue's description and its photographic reproduction of the model seem to deny
de Tolnay's prior identification as a
"Sketch for Hercules" on pp. 15 and
64 in *The Complete Work of
Michelangelo* published in 1965,
and in his *The Art and Thought of
Michelangelo* published in 1964.
The catalogue published in December, 1970, only attributes the model
to Michelangelo, whereas de Tolnay
had formerly adjudged the model,
in these two books to be an
authentic sculpture by Michelangelo.

MODEL OF *ST. JEROME*

(Wax—Fig. 173)

This model in black wax, has in the
past been rejected or ignored by
most art authorities, including
Maclagan, Thode and Goldscheider.

MODEL OF A MALE TORSO

(Terrasecca—Fig. 170)

The catalogue states that the model
is of terracotta, although
Goldscheider, who believes its
authenticity, identifies it as being
of terrasecca.

The numerous small models (approximately nineteen) in wax and clay that
were in the Casa Buonarroti, at the
time that they were examined in 1911
by Sir Eric Maclagan, were according
to him "not very easy to study" and
that as far as he knew "no catalogue
of them, except the list by Dr. Thode,
had ever been published" (*Burlington
Magazine* XLIV, 1924). He further
stated that Dr. Poggi was kind enough
to have the show cases opened for him
and that he was able to examine the
models with Mr. Loeser, Count Carlo
Gamba and Dr. Frizzoni.

The Casa Buonarroti, although

never lived in by the Great Master,
was the home of his nephew, Leonardo,
and his heirs for over three hundred
years. The finest period of the house
was that of Michelangelo's grand-
nephew (Michelangelo Buonarroti the
Younger) who was born four years
after the death of Michelangelo and
died in 1647. During his lifetime he
collected as many relics of his grand-
uncle as he could find and it can be
assumed that many, if not all, of the
nineteen small models in the Casa
Buonarroti were acquired during the
period of the grand-nephew's
lifetime.

Selected Bibliography

ANONYMOUS. in *Die Werkstatt der Kunst,* Leipzig, 1916, Vol. 16, p. 7; AVENARIUS, Ferdinand. "Die Medicikapelle" (Kunstwartverlag Georg D. W. Callwey in Munchen 1911-1914), in *Michelangelo-Mappen des Kunstwart,* 1, (Illustrated); BALDINI, Umberto, et al. *The Complete Work of Michelangelo,* New York, Reynal and Co., 1965; BERLIN. *The Kaiser Friedrich Museum Catalogue,* 1933; BRINCKMANN, A. E. "Terrakotten Michelangelos (?)", in *Repertorium für Kunstwissenschaft,* Vol. 46 (1925), p. 42; BURGER, Fritz. *Studien zu Michelangelo,* Strasburg, Heitz, 1907 (Zur Kunstgeschichte des Auslandes, 49); CASA BUONARROTI, Florence. *Catalogue of the Sculptures of Michelangelo,* December 1970—Charles de Tolnay the Director; DIELITZ, J. "Ein Werk Michel-Angelo's im Königlichen Museum zu Berlin", in *Jahrbucher für Kunstwissenschaft,* Leipzig, 1869, p. 245-249; DONATH, Adolph. "Psychologie des Kunstsammelns", in *Bibliothek für Kunst-und Antiquitaten-Sammler,* Vol. 9, Pichard Carl Schmidt & Co., 1920; GOLDSCHEIDER, Ludwig. *Michelangelo: Paintings, Sculptures, Architecture,* London, Phaidon, reprinted autumn 1963, p. 223: *Michelangelo: Drawings.* (2nd ed.) London, Phaidon, 1966, (Illustration, Plate XVI(b)): *A Survey of Michelangelo's Models in Wax and Clay,* London, Phaidon, 1962 (Illustrated): *Michelangelo's Bozzetti for Statues in the Medici Chapel,* Privately Printed, London, 1957, p. 12; GOTTSCHEWSKI, Adolf. "Ein Original-Tonmodell Michelangelos", in *Munchner Jahrbuch der bildenden Kunst,* Munich, 1906, p. 43-64; GRIMM, Herman. *Leben Michelangelos,* 5th. ed., Berlin, Wilhelm Hertz, 1879, p. 552-553: "Die Sarkophage der Sacristei von San Lorenzo", in *Jahrbuch der Königlichen Preussischen Kunstsammlungen,* Vol. 1, Berlin, 1880, p. 17-29; GROSSE, Julius. *Ernst Julius Haehnel's literarische Reliquien,* Berlin, Grote, 1893; GUTBIER, A. *Katalog* der Michel-Angelo—Ausstellung im Kunst-Ausstellungs-Gebäude auf der Brühl'schen Terrasse zu Dresden. Zur Erinnerung an die 400 jährige Gerburtsfeier Michel-Angelo's, veranstaltet durch Ernst Arnold's Kunsthandlung, Dresden, Lehmann'sche Buchdruckerei, 1875; HAEHNEL, Ernst Julius. *Die Skizzen zu dem Grabmal der Mediceer in Florenz von Hand Michelangelo Buonarrottis gearbeitet: Katalog* Verkäuflicher Kunstgegenstände aus dem Nachlasse; HAMPE, Theodor. *Kunstfreunde im alten Nürnberg und ihre Sammlungen,* Nürnberg, 1903; HARTT, Frederick. *History of Italian Renaissance Art,* Abrams, New York, 1968; HEINEMANN, Hans. "Sechs Terrakotten von Michelangelo in Montreal", in *Weltkunst,* December, 1962, No. 24, p. 11 and 12; HOLMES, Sir Charles J. "A wax model attributed to Michelangelo", in *The Burlington Magazine,* 11, 1907, p. 189-190; HOUSTON, Texas, Museum of Fine Arts. *Catalogue* of Edith A. and Percy S. Strauss Collection, April 1945; JUSTI, Carl. *Michelangelo.* Beiträge zur Erklärung der Werke und des Menschen. Leipzig, Breitkopf & Härtel, 1900; KEYSSLER, Johann Georg. *Neueste Reisen durch Deutschland, Böhmen, Ungarn, die Schweiz, Italien und Lothringen,* Hannover, Nicolai Förster & Sohn, 1751, p. 1409-1410; KNAPP, Friedrich. *Michelangelo,* Stuttgart & Leipzig, Deutsche-Verlags-Anstalt, 1906 (Klassiker der Kunst, 7); LEHNERT, Georg. *Gutachten über Modelle von Michelangelo* (Expert opinion on Models by Michelangelo, May, 1913) Gutachten, erstattet auf Veranlassung des Königlichen Amtsgerichts Berlin

(20 page court transcript); LISNER, M. "Der Kruzifixus Michelangelos im Kloster Santo Spirito in Florenz", in *Kunstchronik,* Vol. 16, 1963; LÜTZOW, Carl von. "Die Michelangelo-Ausstellung in Florenz", in *Zeitschrift für bildende Kunst* 11, Leipzig, 1876, p. 26-29, 94-95 (Illustrations); MACLAGAN, Sir Eric. "The wax models by Michelangelo in the Victoria and Albert Museum", in *The Burlington Magazine,* Vol. 44, 1924, p. 4-16; MEIER-GRAEFE, Julius. *Michelangelo. Die Terrakotten aus der Sammlung Hähnel.* Vierzig auf der Handpresse gedruckte Heliogravüren in der Grösse der Originale. Mit einer Einleitung von Julius Meier-Graefe und dem Ergebnis der Forschungen Henry Thodes. Berlin, Safari-Verlag, 1924 (40 plates); MELLER, Simon. *Michelangelo.* Budapest, Lampel Robert, (1903); MENDELOWITZ, Daniel M. *Study Guide to Drawing* (Revised Edition), New York City, Holt Rinehart & Winston, 1972 (Illustration); 'MICHELANGELO'. "Six small clay sketches by Michelangelo in the LeBrooy Collection", in *Encyclopaedia Britannica,* 1965 and subsequent editions; 'MICHELANGELO'. in *Encyclopaedia of World Art,* Vol. 9, 1964; MIDDLEDORF, Ulrich, and Oswald Goetz. *Catalogue* of Models and Plaquettes from the Sigmund Morgenroth Collection, Art Institute of Chicago Exhibition, 1944; MÜNTZ, Eugène. "Les collections d'antiques formées par les Médicis au XVIe siècle", in *Mémoire de l'Académie des inscriptions et belles-lettres,* Vol. 35, Paris, 1895; MURR, Christophe Theophile. *Description du Cabinet de monsieur Paul de Praun à Nuremberg,* Nuremberg, J. Theophile Schneider, 1797; PFISTER, Kurt. "Die Terrakotten Michelangelos", in *Deutsche Kunst und Dekoration,* 1924, Vol. 55, p. 305 (Illustrations); POPE-HENNESSY, Sir John. *Catalogue of Italian Sculpture in the Victoria and Albert Museum,* Vol. 2 and 3, London, Phaidon, 1968 (Illustrations); POPP, A. E. *Die Medici-Kapelle Michelangelos,* Munich, O. C. Recht, 1922; SCHOTTMÜLLER, Frida. "Tonstatuette nach der Medicimadonna (früher im Praunschen Kabinett in Nürnberg) no. 351", in *Königliche Museen zu Berlin,* Berlin, Georg Reimer, 1913, Vol. 5; SPRINGER, Anton. "Raffael und Michelangelo", in *Kunst und Künstler des Mittelalters und der Neuzeit,* Edited by Robert Dohme, 2, Abtheilung, Leipzig, E. A. Seemann, 1878, Vol. 2, p. 245-264; STEINMANN, Ernst. *Das Geheimnis der Medicigräber Michelangelos,* Leipzig, K. W. Hiersemann, 1907 (Kunstgeschichtliche Monographien, 4): "Michelangelo-Modelle", in *Cicerone,* Vol. 16 (1924), p. 991-995; THODE, Henry. "Michelangelos Tonmodelle aus der Hähnelschen Sammlung", in *Monatshefte für Kunstwissenschaft,* Vol. 6 (Leipzig 1913), p. 309-317 (Illustrations): "Michelangelo. Kritische Untersuchungen über seine Werke", 1908-1913 supplements to *Michelangelo und das Ende der Renaissance,* Vols. 4, 5, 6, Berlin, G. Grote, 1902-1913, Vol. 6, p. 309-317 (p. 265-286 of Vol. 6 gives an incomplete 'catalogue' of models attributed to Michelangelo); TOLNAY, Charles de. *The Medici Chapel,* Princeton, 1948: *The Complete Work of Michelangelo* (by other authors also), New York, Reynal and Co., 1965: *The Art and Thought of Michelangelo,* New York, Pantheon, 1964; VANCOUVER, British Columbia, Canada. *Catalogue* of Six Models by Michelangelo in the LeBrooy Collection in Vancouver; VASARI, Giorgio. *Lives of the most eminent painters, sculptors, and architects,* Translated from the Italian of Georgio Vasari, by Jonathan Foster, London, Henry G. Bohn, 1850, 5 vol.

Acknowledgments

The colour photographs of the terracotta models of "Dawn" and of "Night", as well as that of "The right hand of Moses" and "The right arm of Christ in the Pietà" are reproduced by kind permission of the Victoria and Albert Museum, London. The colour photographs of the terracotta model of "Day" are reproduced by kind permission of the Museum of Fine Arts, Houston. The photographs of the terracotta model of the "Medici Madonna" are reproduced by kind permission of the Staatliche Museum, Berlin; the photographs of the models, Figs. 4, 7, 9, 10, 133, 159, 169, 170, 172 and 173 by kind permission of the Casa Buonarroti, Florence. The photographs of the two models, Figs. 135 and 171 are reproduced by kind permission of the British Museum, London. Geoffrey Traunter, the designer of this volume, merits the author's sincere thanks for the results of his lengthy and difficult undertaking. The excellent design of this book could only have been achieved in its present form by a very knowledgeable designer, who is also a professional artist and teacher, and therefore able to impart a remarkable sensitivity into the 'design concept', thus portraying a true appreciation of the subject matter of the manuscript presented to him. Grateful acknowledgment is due to Ernest Harrison of Vancouver for the perfection of his colour photographs of the Canadian Collection. J. Eugene Horvath and his wife Maria, of Vancouver, were very helpful with certain very important aspects of this book. W. J. Luetticken of Montreal and Hardwin von Hahn and Frederick Sholz, both of Vancouver, were kind enough to translate from German into English many portions of the great amount of research material acquired from German sources. Acknowledgment is also due Anthony Blicq, the Director of the University of British Columbia Press, for his advice and encouragement with respect to the publication of the manuscript. Finally, the author wishes to express his sincere gratitude to his wife, Phyllis, and to his twin brother, Peter — without whose encouragement, advice and valuable assistance this volume would not have been completed.

Index

Overleaf:
The Sistine Chapel, Rome. Part of the "Ceiling Fresco" and
"The Last Judgment" on the altar wall of the Chapel.

Designer: Geoffrey Traunter. Editor: John Houghton
Colour photography (Can. Coll.): Commercial Illustrators Ltd.,
Vancouver, British Columbia
Typesetting: Photype Centre Ltd., Vancouver, British Columbia
Printed and bound in Canada by Evergreen Press Limited,
Vancouver, British Columbia.